HOW I FAKED MY OWN DEATH
AND DID *NOT* GET AWAY WITH IT

HOW I FAKED MY OWN DEATH
AND DID *NOT* GET AWAY WITH IT

A TRUE STORY

HARRY GORDON

This edition published in 2021 by New Holland Publishers
Sydney • Auckland

Level 1, 178 Fox Valley Road, Wahroonga, NSW 2076, Australia
5/39 Woodside Ave, Northcote, Auckland 0627, New Zealand

newhollandpublishers.com

First published in 2007 by New Holland Publishers
as *The Harry Gordon Story: How I Faked My Own Death*

A record of this book is held at the National Library of Australia.

ISBN 9781760794071

Group Managing Director: Fiona Schultz
Publisher: Lesley Pagett
Project Editor: Liz Hardy
Designer: Andrew Davies
Production Director: Arlene Gippert
Printed in China

10 9 8 7 6 5 4 3 2 1

Keep up with New Holland Publishers:

 NewHollandPublishers

 @newhollandpublishers

Some of the names in this book have been changed.

Dedicated
to David Collon

CONTENTS

1

The disappearance

JUNE 2000

The winter sun had long since set over the deserted waters of the Karuah estuary, east of the Hunter Valley in New South Wales, Australia. Darkness was falling quickly. There were no other boats in sight, no sign of life on the uninhabited shore where the trees had already merged into an indistinct blur.

When I switched off the motor there was a brief sloshing sound, as my 'quickboat' lost its momentum. Then there was nothing but silence. The last gentle gliding motion washed the boat up to a channel marker post that I had aimed for. I quickly slipped a rope around the marker, hitched the rope to a rail and settled back to relax. There was no sound or movement of any kind; in that huge expanse of water I was quite alone. I poured myself another glass of champagne from the open bottle then telephoned my daughter on her mobile phone. She had left the yacht club after a Saturday winter series race but was still in

Sydney with places to go and things to do before she would even start her journey up to our North Arm Cove home.

She said that by the time she finished all her errands then drove the 250 kilometres to North Arm Cove it would probably be well after 11 o'clock. Then she asked what I was up to.

'I am still on my way back from an excellent seafood lunch at Zacs Restaurant in Karuah,' I explained. 'The outboard motor has broken down, nothing serious, probably dirty fuel. I will just have to clean the intake jets.'

I had been out on my boat for much of the day, south of my home in Port Stephens. I had returned briefly to my house earlier, before proceeding north up the Karuah River in the afternoon for lunch. During my brief stop at my house I made some basic preparations in case I did really decide to go through with my plan. I loaded some clothing, odds and ends, plus a bag with $100,000 cash into a VW campervan. I drove the van to a public parking space at the other end of my street. I walked through a bush shortcut to my home and onto my private wharf to continue my day on the water.

'Are you safe Dad?' Josaphine asked in a concerned voice.

'I am perfectly safe,' I replied. 'The boat is tied to a marker post in perfectly calm water in the Karuah Estuary; I could paddle to the shore from here if I needed to.'

She asked some minor follow up questions until she was satisfied then we gossiped a bit before exchanging mutual declarations of love, as was our habit, then the telephone call ended. My message had been reasonably obscure and everybody processes information differently, but I felt sure that on reflection the message that 'I would be all right no matter what happened' would give her the assurance she would need for what was to follow.

I finished the glass of champagne, poured myself another,

then sat back with my feet up to relax and reflect on my next move. 'Shall I do this or not? It's not too late to change your mind,' I said out loud. 'This will probably end badly!'

Then ignoring my own sensible advice I emptied my glass of champagne overboard before starting out on the biggest journey of my life.

First I removed the rubber dinghy from under its cover, inflated it with the foot pump then slid it over the side and secured it. Next, I lent over the side and fitted my brand new, tiny outboard motor to the rubber dinghy before throwing the foot pump, torch and carry bag into it.

I moved quickly about the boat, overturning loose items to simulate the effect of the boat having run into something at speed. Next I disconnected the fuel tank, drained the remaining fuel, reconnected it then started the boat's large outboard motor and ran it for a couple of minutes until it ran out of fuel and spluttered to a stop.

I looked around the cockpit, where my mobile phone and wallet containing credit cards and cash sat on the dashboard where they would remain. All around me were commonplace items, all familiar and personal. I knew I would never see them again and felt a twinge of loss. I unhitched the rope from the channel marker post allowing the boat to float free with the tide before slipping myself over the side and into the rubber dinghy.

The little 1hp outboard motor didn't start on the first five pulls. 'Oh dear!' I said to myself anxiously. 'This journey could be over before it even starts if I don't have a getaway boat.' The outboard motor came alive on the sixth pull and using the rubber dinghy as a sort of tug boat I shunted the 'quickboat' into the shoreline. To my dismay when I reached the shore I found that the little outboard motor didn't have enough power to shunt the quickboat hard aground. 'Oh dear!' I said again as

I slipped myself over the side waist deep in the cold water. 'This wasn't in the script.'

I pushed the 'quickboat' hard aground by hand then heaved myself back into the rubber dinghy – it seemed to be smaller than I remembered it. It felt unstable and unsafe. The little outboard motor wouldn't start again. 'I don't know that my heart can take this,' I said to myself, but on the sixth pull it started once again.

Running at about half throttle, I steered the rubber dinghy towards one of the flashing red channel marker posts as I shivered miserably with the cold. As the dinghy left the calm estuary waters and entered the exposed waters of Port Stephens, the wind picked up and the water turned lumpy. As the last channel marker of the estuary faded behind me, the only visible light ahead was a faint white light glimmering from the oyster farm island in the distance.

'It's a moonless night,' I chided myself. 'It's mid-winter, you have never been in these waters at night before, you have no chart, so even if you do finally see shore lights you have no way of knowing where you are. You are in a tiny rubber dinghy with a tiny little fuel tank that may last you an hour or so before running out of fuel, then you will be in an open waterway with no power, you could die here tonight you know. You really didn't think this through did you? You are a very, very foolish man.'

As it happened, running at half throttle it took two hours to finally reach my destination and there was still a little fuel left in the tank when I arrived. I had been lost and in despair several times during the voyage but at last I switched off the motor and glided into the deserted beach. Shivering with fear and cold, I pulled the dinghy up on the beach well clear of the water line, disconnected the outboard motor then stiff with cold and cramp I hobbled up the beach with it before laying it down quietly next to my campervan. I went back down the beach and returned with the dinghy and remaining odds and ends. I paused, took a deep breath, then opened the side door of the campervan, shoved in the dinghy and the outboard motor, slammed the side door shut swung open the door and slid into the driver's seat in a single movement. The motor burst into life with the typical, deafening Volkswagen clatter that could wake the dead. Thankfully no lights came on in the nearby houses as I selected first gear, gunned the engine and clattered away. 'The getaway vehicle was certainly an inspired choice wasn't it?', I mumbled to myself.

At least the Volkswagen's heater could blow warming hot air on me. Within 20 minutes my teeth were still chattering and I continued to shake, probably more from anxiety than from the cold. I remembered the money in the back and stopped to check it was still there – another risk taken. Fortunately, it was still there.

The drive seemed to take forever, but actually less than two hours passed before the Caltex roadhouse on the freeway to Sydney came into view. I pulled the campervan into the truck stop area and parked it in front of two large truck and trailer rigs that were overnighting there. I slipped myself into the back, out of my wet clothes and quickly into bed. Despite the enormity of all that had happened I was exhausted and fell into a deep dreamless sleep almost immediately.

In the morning I slid out of bed, dressed myself, deflated the dinghy and stowed both it and the outboard motor into storage compartments in the van. I hung up all the clothing from an overnight bag then fussed about in the van until everything seemed tidy and shipshape. I looked longingly at the roadhouse and considered going in for a hot breakfast of bacon and eggs but decided, on balance, that it was too risky. I drove away hungry but thankfully now warm and dry.

Right there and then I knew I had made a huge mistake. I wanted to go back to my former life but I knew that it was already too late. 'This is a huge mistake, why are you doing this Harry? You don't even have a plan, this can only end badly', I said out loud to myself as the Volkswagen campervan clattered down the freeway to Sydney.

When I arrived at the St Ives turn-off on the North Shore, I turned left and drove across to the Northern Beaches and turned left again. Along the way I stopped at a fast food outlet and bought some fish and chips then I stopped again at a liquor store for a couple of bottles of champagne. At last I parked at Palm Beach and looked out to the ocean and ate the first meal of my new life as I sipped champagne. With the hot food in my stomach and feeling slightly light-headed from the champagne much of the tension washed away from me.

'You can do this Harry, it's not for the faint-hearted but you can do it,' I told myself. I drove to the nearest shopping centre supermarket and bought some groceries, then made my way to a beach camping ground. As I expected the camping ground was almost empty in mid-winter so I had no problem at all securing a vacant site.

The man on reception duty was so involved with his computer screen that he hardly even looked at me as he issued me a receipt then recited directions without even thinking about what he was saying. It was obvious that I was of no interest to him. 'So far so good,' I said to myself as I clattered the Volkswagen down to the nominated site.

There were a few caravans and tents dotted sparsely here about the grounds in no particular pattern that I could detect and I was relieved to find that I had no immediate neighbours on either side of my particular site. None of the people took the slightest interest in me and I felt quite safe and secure. I worked out how to plug in the mains power cable to the box provided. I then found a good hiding place for the money in a panel in the campervan. After shaving I luxuriated in a long hot soapy shower in one of the communal shower blocks and walked through the camping grounds and along the waterfront. Later, as dinner was cooking on the little campervan stove and I poured myself another glass of champagne I smugly remarked to myself. 'Ah, this is the life.' I had never, ever been camping in my life before. This was all new to me. I had always been a hotel man and this was starting to feel like a real adventure holiday.

In the morning I felt as bright as a button. I shaved and showered and with a real spring in my step I walked out of the camping ground and down the road to a small block of shops. 'What an excellent morning!' I remarked to the young Asian shop assistant behind the counter of the first shop I entered and bought a few items, fresh bread rolls, newspapers and some butter before strolling back to the campervan.

With hot coffee and a bread roll dripping with butter and jam I opened the newspaper. There on page three of the newspaper was a quarter page article about my disappearance with a photo of me that was a very good likeness. 'This is bad, very, very bad,' I muttered. Just a few minutes ago I had been carefree and in high spirits but now I felt dangerously exposed. I peeked out the windows of the campervan, half expecting the staff, other campers, perhaps even the police to come rushing up to me and say: 'Isn't this you?'

As I looked out the window, there was nobody rushing up to the campervan, nobody was interested in me, all was quiet, it was really hard to believe.

Those first weeks were very tense. The newspaper coverage

seemed relentless and when the weekend came there were huge photos of me in the Sunday papers and so much copy; goodness knows why, I was not a public figure, I was just a Sydney businessman.

'What the hell is all this about?' I asked myself. 'Fishermen get washed off the rocks all the time and blokes drown when their boats turn over, heck they don't get this sort of publicity, what is this all about?'

The media seemed to make a lot of the fact that I was a millionaire. 'Gosh, it's not as if I am a tycoon or anything, anyone of my age who has a reasonable size business and a decent freehold home is a millionaire,' I said to myself. 'What an earth are they going on about?'

The exposure was so relentless that I felt certain I would be discovered. In those first weeks I wore a hat and sunglasses as I shuttled between various camping grounds. When there was a lull in the newspaper coverage I slipped down to Kensington in Sydney's eastern suburbs and into a tiny flat I rented. I paid cash with no questions asked, using the name Bill Teare.

The little flat was in a dilapidated block of flats where most of the other tenants were Middle Eastern and Asian people who had no interest in socialising with me. It allowed me to settle anonymously and find my feet. I knew that in due course I would be able to make contact with my wife Sheila to resolve our future, but in the meantime I needed to maintain the lowest profile I could.

In the first month after my 'disappearance', despite my best efforts to keep a low profile I still had face to face speaking contact with more than 20 people. I often wore a hat and sometimes glasses, but it seemed to me at the time to be nothing short of a miracle that nobody recognised me. I was pleased that my short-lived camping adventure was well and truly behind me and I happily settled into my little Kensington flat and changed my routine.

One of the first things I did was to buy a bicycle for myself. Kensington is just a few kilometres from downtown Sydney so the bicycle provided me with a quick cost effective commute without any parking problems. I decided that until my future was resolved with Sheila I would spend some time on creative writing to put some much needed structure back in my daily life. I resolved to spend some time reading then learning to write poetry, to develop better prose, then I would attempt to write short stories. I didn't know how long it would take to even meet with Sheila but however long it took I knew I would never get disposable free time like this again in my life so it was important to extract as much value as I could from it, rather than just let it drift by.

Each morning, like millions of other people, I would shave, shower then eat a small breakfast before bicycling into the Aquatic Centre in Park Street, Sydney. After swimming 50 laps of the pool I would bicycle down to the NSW Public Library in Macquarie Street to start my creative writing time. I immersed myself in Tennyson, Yates and Kipling for a full month before starting to write a simple poem each week for myself. Six words to a line, four lines to a verse with the rhyme in the second and fourth line, four verses per poem. I was worse than hopeless. I would never be able to write a simple poem for a Hallmark card.

Before starting with my short stories I turned my attention to Shakespeare, *Richard III, Hamlet, Othello* then *Macbeth*. Neither Shakespeare nor Tolstoy helped me, they both just made me feel inadequate but at long last I started to write. I set myself a target of 3,000 words a week, 600 a day but by the time I edited my work the final output was closer to 600 words per week. At least I was engaged in writing, not just drifting through time.

After my morning swim and creative reading and writing I would slip out of the library at about one o'clock to buy myself a sandwich for my lunch. I would normally walk through Hyde Park, pausing to eat my sandwich on a park bench. Then I would make my way to the Art Gallery of NSW where, on average, I would spend about an hour each day. My favourite painting was and still is *The Queen of Sheba meets King Solomon* by Sir Edward Poynter but in fact after spending so much time with them many of the old masters became firm friends that I looked forward to visiting with them each day. I also spent time absorbing many of the large nineteenth century New World landscape paintings. I really only enjoy the great outdoors when it is captured on canvas and I am standing in air conditioning. I never enjoyed hiking in the real great outdoors with the heat and flies, so art is the only way for me to really get involved with it. As it happens, I am exactly the opposite with the naked female form – I rather like looking at the naked body of my lover, but nudes on canvas leave me cold. I find them vaguely embarrassing for some reason. After my art gallery visit each day I would bicycle home to my little flat and write until about six o'clock in the evening.

Some evenings I would walk to the local bottle shop to buy a cold bottle of champagne, then return home to cook myself dinner and settle in for the evening.

As had been my habit for many years I continued to go to the cinema in George Street Sydney each Tuesday night and at least once a week to a live show, the opera maybe, perhaps a play or to the comedy club to give myself a laugh. Adopting the theory that all work and no play would make me a very dull person I did not work on weekends, not even housework, it was strictly playtime. I often spent Saturday or Sunday at the seaside, different beaches every time with lunchtime feasts of fish and chips for a special treat.

I took ferry trips to Manly, delighting again to have the feel of water movement under my feet, the smell of the ocean and the salty sea breeze against my face. I even spent the odd weekend out of town in the campervan, including two days at the War Memorial Museum in Canberra. Thus my life settled into a new and steady routine of work and play. I was writing – however slowly and badly I was at last writing. I found that I didn't miss my business life at all although I did miss the companionship of friends at work. Most of all I missed my daughter Josaphine and my wife Sheila. To my surprise I missed sex more than I had expected – much more than sex I just missed the physical contact. It was a big gap in my life.

'I am going to try and work my way through this stuff,' I had told her before she left for Egypt. 'But if I can't and I have to disappear I will be in contact with you in about three months but no later than six months. If you don't hear from me within six months you can assume I am dead, claim the life insurance and just get on with your life.'

Sheila hadn't taken any of it seriously. 'Oh, fuck off!' she replied laughingly. 'You will work your way through the problems, you always do, and how could you leave this magnificent body?' she asked wiggling her recently enhanced breasts.

On my third outing to the George Street cinema, just a month after my 'disappearance', I had my first unplanned encounter with my past. Like most people, I had a working relationship with about 150 to 200 people, but outside that I knew perhaps 500 to 1000 more of past clients, old employees, subcontractors, their spouses, old suppliers, people I met at social, political and commercial functions. People who I have seen but I don't remember their names.

I had my ticket and an ice cream in my right hand as I wandered through the lobby from the ticket counter to the theatre door passage when I noticed her blinking nervously at me about 20 metres away. She was about 45 years old, very attractive with bright green eyes and very black hair. Well groomed with a floaty dress and classy accessories, she was in fact quite a picture. Now she started walking towards me as if she knew me. Flight was pointless, so with my heart pounding I braced myself.

'It's you isn't it?' she asked earnestly, grasping my arm so firmly that my ice cream was at risk.

'Well it certainly was me, in an earlier life,' I confirmed with my warmest smile.

'But now I am someone else, in a witness protection program, the person you knew died I'm afraid.'

The unrehearsed explanation sounded silly as it came out of my mouth, like the line from a third rate actor in a B-grade movie. Why didn't I think and rehearse an intelligent explanation, I wondered as I smiled at her. Surely a meeting like this was always possible. Strangely she didn't seem to notice how disingenuous the explanation was.

'Oh, oh, I see, how awful for you!,' she said wrinkling her nose with genuine concern.

'Shouldn't you be in another country or at least in another state?,' she asked earnestly. She was fully and deliciously fragranced and at that least appropriate moment I swooned slightly in her company, becoming aware of her breasts and her femininity and without conscious thought I moved closer to her until we were almost touching.

'Yes, of course, and I will be relocated in due course but in the meantime they need me here in Sydney to make statements for evidence.'

I lowered my voice to almost a whisper. 'I am not really supposed to be out and about you know. I sneaked out of the safe house for a movie to give myself a little break from it all.'

Does your wife know about this?' she asked in a whisper.

'No she doesn't, she will just have to move on and make a new life,' I replied.

'How awful,' she replied but her expression indicated she was not displeased at all. She obviously knew us but felt no sympathy for Sheila, perhaps she didn't even like Sheila. She searched my face for almost a minute, then seeming satisfied she continued.

'Don't worry; your secret is safe with me.'

She kissed me on the cheek then wafted off to join a girlfriend. I didn't know who she was then and I don't know to this day but I do know that her word was good. The secret was safe with her and it was also safe with several other people I met in Sydney that year by chance, none of them close personal friends. It was quite amazing that after I said 'Witness protection program.' very few asked personal or awkward questions. They all seemed very kind, sympathetic and helpful.

Although my life had settled into a safe, steady and secure routine I was aware that it was a temporary life. I calculated that at my current rate of frugal expenditure the cash reserve I had on me could last another two years but by that time I would be flat broke and all out of options. I firmly resolved to limit my current life to no more than one year. By June 2001, the anniversary of my disappearance, I would need to be running with a new plan. Could I return to my old life? I wondered. That was doubtful, but if not I would need to create a new life where I generated income and constructed wealth again. Very soon it would be time for me to make contact with Sheila again and although I missed her and missed married life I wasn't looking forward to what I knew would be a difficult meeting.

I had taken a huge leap of faith with Sheila and now she controlled all our assets, our cash reserves, including the slush fund, our income, everything. She was the keeper now.

•••••

I suppose I had come to accept that all women are probably a bit odd. In fact it seemed to me that part of growing up was learning to accept that women were very different from men, that was just life! My mother had always seemed irrational and more than a bit odd. Both of my sisters could be awkward, irrational and were quite strange in some of their behaviours. My wife Sheila was even more different than most but I didn't understand how much or why. That information took years to seep into my consciousness. In the beginning she just seemed to be a bit highly strung and a real handful like my sister True. There was nothing wrong with that in my opinion.

There were hints in our early time together but the first real proof that there was a problem came to me just before our daughter Josaphine was born in January 1975. It was typical Auckland weather for that time of year, warm but not yet really hot. Sheila was in distress and felt an overwhelming urge to throw herself out the third floor window of St Helens Maternity Hospital. I put my arms around her and spoke softly, soothing words of love and reason but in reality I didn't understand or relate to her feelings at all. I felt insincere, like a third rate actor in a play. Had I really left Wendy for this unattractive creature? Perhaps she would jump. I considered the scenario. I would be rid of her without any guilt. Wendy would probably take me back.

As these thoughts ran through my mind loving, soothing words of reason continued to flow from me, washing over her until at last the crisis was past and the madness subsided. The next day our daughter Josaphine was born. 'Welcome to the world my little daughter,' I greeted her.

I hadn't expected to love Josaphine. Much of my emotional life with Sheila prior to the birth had been emotionally shallow but I loved Josaphine from the moment I saw her.

She wasn't a cute baby. To call her ugly would have been too harsh but her fat little face and strange hair were certainly unfortunate. I loved her then and I love her now. My life with Sheila often required fraudulent displays of emotion but Josaphine has always been an enduring connection with emotional reality.

To leave Sheila now would be to leave Josaphine and that was unthinkable, I would have to make it work.

In the early years of our marriage Sheila had managed to hide her erratic nature from me. It wasn't hard as I certainly wasn't on a quest to discover new problems. I had learned that with each new 'coming out' of one of her behaviours my acceptance allowed that behaviour or belief to become normal within family life. In June 1983, I was about to take Josaphine to a GFS meeting, a sort of Anglican Girl Guides organisation. It was early evening as we walked downstairs to the basement garage. Sheila appeared at the top of the stairs, eyes ablaze with rage, shouting at us. Further paroxysms of rage continued as we walked into the garage but the sounds coming out were not identifiable words.

Josaphine sat in silence, seeming tiny in the passenger seat as we drove away, waiting for me to open the conversation.

'Sometimes your mother is not quite herself. She doesn't seem well, sometimes.' There, in that seminal moment, for the very first time I had spoken out loud to Josaphine about her mother's behaviour and there was no way for me to withdraw the words now. It was of course cowardly to attack Sheila behind her back without giving her the opportunity to defend herself. There would have been more decency to have spoken the words in front of her, but it was too late now and from that day onwards father and daughter would manage Shiela together, like an endless evening with a drunk who won't go to bed.

This was the same wife in whom I had placed all my trust when I started my journey of survival in June 2000. We may have had 25 years of marriage together, but allowing her to be my only lifeline was a huge leap of faith.

Before returning to her I needed to review all the reasons for my journey. Were they all still valid? Had they ever been valid or was I caught up in some irrational paranoia? We would need to jointly decide what should happen next and it is fair to say that I had some misgivings.

2

The pressures to disappear

1999

I think it was in late 1998 or early 1999 when Alek first telephoned me. 'Hello, hello again to you Harry,' his deep voice boomed. 'This is Alek, perhaps your thinking will remember me?'

The voice and slightly muddled accent were indeed familiar, as was Ukrainian Alek. He was about 45 years old, tall, handsome with jet-black hair, a huge moustache and bright twinkling blue eyes behind old fashioned steel rimmed glasses. He was larger than life, charming and charismatic, I remembered him instantly with pleasure. In 1997 I had been on a one-week industry course at Monash University and remembered chatting with Alek several times during coffee breaks as he was taking a similar course at the same time. He had been entertaining company and I smiled with pleasure on hearing his voice. '*Previet Alek, kakdewaa?*' (Hello Alek, how are things?) I responded with the only couple of words in broken Russian I could remember.

'Harry, can I be visiting your office in Botany for an hour anytime this week to be talking some business with you? Your French and Russian are hopeless,' he laughed, 'we will make our business in English yes?'

At the time I thought that he probably wanted to sell pumps to one of our businesses and was pleased to make an appointment with him to call on me the next day. When he arrived, to my surprise he told me that he wasn't calling to sell me pumps and in fact he already understood that his range of small pumps were unsuited to our heavy industrial applications.

'No, Harry, I have been thinking about your concepts in the conversations we were having about modern maintenance systems, you have been making a deep impression on my thinking and I have been talking with some business associates who are soon visiting Australia. We would the very much liking if you to give a two to three hour formal presentation on your systems. We are shortly to starting in the papermaking business in the Ukraine, no conflicting of interest with your clients, this will be a favour from you to me and of course we will pay you a fee. Please to say yes Harry.'

I was flattered, and agreed setting a date with him for the following month. From memory, I think we set a fee of $2,000 but it was incidental really, I probably would have done it for nothing.

On the day, my three-hour presentation with visual aids was a huge success. I was quite magnificent, informative and entertaining. I had even sprinkled a few Russian words into my presentation. They were most impressed and pressed me into 30 hours of intense follow-on meetings over the next two days about modern paper mill maintenance with particular focus on bearing analysis through noise and heat monitoring.

I learned that the core business of this group had been a

pump manufacturing business north of Kurskaya, but through associate companies they were rapidly growing by acquiring government-owned businesses during a political period when all previous communist governments in Eastern Europe were privatising industry and commerce. Their latest target was a cardboard box manufacturer including a small feeder paper mill. They had identified that the current cost of maintenance within the target business was running at about 200 per cent above world best practice, so a step change in maintenance methods would be required as part of a general restructuring in order to make the business profitable.

I was surprised and elated when they invited me to join the board of the takeover company with a 7 per cent shareholding in exchange for my input within restructuring of the maintenance systems.

'What a stroke of luck in my career,' I thought. I just happened to be in the right place at the right time, what a breakthrough this was for me. The takeover was to be financed with 100 per cent debt so no up front capital was required from any of the parties, but they made it very clear that we would need to restructure the business very quickly as the finance arrangements did not allow us to trade unprofitably for very long. We entered into a Heads of Agreement on the spot with strict secrecy provisions on all parties until the takeover was completed.

My own small personal holding company, Patterson & Gordon Pty Ltd, committed to owning the seven per cent shareholding in the takeover company and my directorship in the takeover company required me to commit to three months at the Ukrainian paper mill site within 10 days of the takeover completion and thereafter no less than three months every year for the next five years.

There was no doubt that if the takeover was successful this new venture was going to absorb 25 per cent of my time, and require huge changes in the way I organised my personal and commercial life. It was all very heady stuff. There were warm hugs with kisses on both cheeks all round as we said our final farewells at the airport four days later. We all wished ourselves luck over vodka toasts in the bar and congratulated each other on the new relationship and the venture together. Then they were gone.

I had spent almost a week of meetings on the project so after their departure it took a full two weeks to catch up with my normal commercial workload. I was so excited at the prospects this deal would bring, it was the big breakthrough I needed to take me to an entirely different level of wealth. I would have liked to have discussed it with some of my existing business associates but the deal had been done in the strictest confidence.

It was too good to be true, but floating along in a cloud of my own greed and ego I believed it all.

Some weeks later the final paperwork arrived by courier, all typed in Russian so Alek guided me through it. Apart from Patterson and Gordon Pty Ltd's obligations I also had to sign director's guarantees for the bank loans, all normal but a bit frightening given the sums of money involved.

'Gosh if the takeover succeeds then the business fails I will really finished,' I mentioned to Alek. 'Me too, my friend,' he replied, 'This really is the big timing for us isn't it?'

About two months later, Alek contacted me to call at his office and sign some additional security documents that were required by the bank. These documents had been prepared in both Russian and English. They required the additional security of our personal family real estate, owned in my wife's name, and company guarantees from the other companies in which

I was a director and held minority shareholding. I recoiled from the prospect with disbelief. All our personal real estate was owned in my wife's name for the very reason of protecting it in case I lost everything in a catastrophic business loss. The other company guarantees would have been quite illegal and just out of the question.

When I explained this to Alek he was charming in response. 'Harry, Harry my friend you are worrying too much, this is a Ukrainian bank, I too must guarantee with my house, who will ever know, what will it matter, they couldn't call the security even if they want to, it's just a formality, it's a wonderful deal, we will all be rich yes? We are almost done in this deal, not so much to worry, yes?'

But it was a worry; in fact, by this time it smelt like a scam to me and I didn't really know what sort of scam it was and how far I was in it.

'You are going to have to give me some time with this one Alek, I will need a month. I just can't commit to this on the spot, perhaps there is a better way with less risk, a win, win outcome.' Alek said I didn't have a month; the deadline was two weeks for it to be signed off. 'Harry, Harry, my good friend you do understanding that this is a serious thing, yes? We are already partners in this thing, the bid has been made, serious money has already been spent, it is too late to stop, yes? This is serious Harry!'

I telephoned him exactly seven days later. 'Alek, this is Harry. I can't do what is being asked, I just can't, it's as simple as that. I am sincerely sorry for any problems that this may bring to the bid but I didn't agree to this Alek, I was asked to join the board and take a shareholding on the basis of my specialist skills. Now if the team needs to replace me, if I loose my directorship and equity participation I will understand, whatever the team needs is all right with me and I am still happy to help with the restructure in a consultancy capacity.'

'Oh Harry my friend,' Alek replied in a slow, deep and deliberate voice. 'You must understand, what you are speaking will damage me but I am an unimportant person. Harry our partners are important and serious people, what you are speaking will damage them as if you were planning to stab them with a knife and they will damage you back Harry, in a physical way, for God's sake Harry, as your friend I tell you that you must worries for your safety, I tell you my friend Ukraine is not like Australia, these are serious people, do you understanding me Harry?' Oh I understood him all right and it sent a chill right through me, this threat was about as raw and basic as it could be.

Several days later as I left the office I was caught and bundled into a car by three burly young men I had never seen before. In a quiet courtyard two of them stood watching as one beat me quickly and wordlessly, all the blows to my body, none to my face, I was shocked and frightened more than injured, as they had intended I suppose.

'Harry, I am so sorry it has come to this, these people are nothing to do with me, I am not controlling any of this and I can't help you but I am telling you it will get worse if you don't fix it, this thing may kill you!,' Alek said to me on the telephone the next day. He was right, it did get worse, much worse, the next time I was taken away, the beating was more savage and I cried without dignity of any kind. I called Alek the same night.

'Alek what has been asked of me was never part of the agreement and now with this savagery we have passed a point where I could ever participate as part of the team, you must understand that, I'm out Alek, of course I am willing to pay compensation, if it is fair, reasonable, if I can afford it, if it is detailed in writing as a proper legal document that allows me to claim the cost as a commercial expense that will pass a tax audit. It's over Alek, I give up, let's just end this quietly.'

Alek said very little, but it was clear that it was just about money. He said he would come back to me. I had bought some time and set out a process to buy myself out of the mess. I had changed direction and provided myself with a pathway forward. Alek was right. This was a very serious matter. Driven by my own greed and ego I had already made a serious error of judgment to get myself into this mess. I had to now proceed carefully – if I made another error, or if they made an error before the concluding deal was done I could be killed. This was much bigger than money. I was going to need some life insurance, just in case, and I would need to brief my wife Sheila, she would need to be involved anyway if we were going to increase our overdraft and I estimated that this was probably going to cost between $150,000 to $250,000 to settle.

I didn't tell Sheila about the beatings, I was too ashamed I suppose. It seemed so unmanly to be beaten without even fighting back but I did tell her about the rest, including the death threat.

'Tell them we won't pay them a fucking penny.' That was Sheila's position – always brave, always ready to take a fight on, head on. This was going to be hard, her whites were always white, her blacks always black and this particular deal was going to have to be concluded in the grey in between.

This couldn't have come at a worse time in our relationship, now that we had the storm cloud of Lisa hanging over us. Ah yes, Lisa was another really big problem.

In mid-1999 I had been standing in a hot and dusty disused concrete plant in Western Sydney, watching but not actively supervising one of our dismantling crews preparing to lift down the cement feed silo. The 70-tonne crane was connected and was starting to take the weight of the silo as the crew removed the last of the connecting bolts from the supporting platform. It was at this delicate stage of the job that my mobile phone rang. 'Hi, this is Harry,' I answered with my customary greeting.

'Is that Mr Gordon who lived in Tauranga, New Zealand in 1965 and had a girlfriend named Claire?' a female voice asked.

'Yes I did,' I replied, without knowing where this conversation was leading.

'Mr Gordon, my name is Lisa, you don't know me but I believe you are my father. Claire became pregnant in 1966 and her baby was adopted out. That baby was me. A few years ago Claire found me, we have regular contact. Claire is my birth mother and she says you are my birth father.' Her voice fell expectantly silent.

Well! That wasn't a telephone call I had been expecting but I knew in an instant that my initial response would be very important to this woman who was obviously on a voyage of personal discovery.

'How wonderful!' I paused then continued. 'I remember Claire well, she is a good and truthful person, if she told you I am your father she will be correct. Wow! Another daughter, this is wonderful news.'

I could almost hear her relief as we chatted away. No, her love of horses didn't come from me, no I didn't have big blue eyes like her, as a matter of fact although the conversation flowed easily between us it was apparent that we didn't have a lot in common except the obvious. We exchanged addresses, we agreed to write to one another and I issued an open invitation to her to visit me anytime.

The phone call ended and without pausing for reflection I telephoned Sheila who, by coincidence, happened to be in New Zealand visiting her sister at that time, as she often did.

I told her about the telephone call. Responding to an outburst of anger I assured her it had nothing to do with our marriage. Claire and I had been young teenage lovers having a summer romance many years before our marriage. There was no issue of me being an unfaithful husband. Once that was cleared up Sheila's anger turned on Lisa.

'What the fuck does she want after all these years?,' she demanded. I explained that to the best of my knowledge Lisa didn't appear to be seeking anything more than an understanding of her biological history. She had made it clear that she was not seeking money and certainly not a father. She was a married woman with a husband and two children of her own. Her adoptive father and mother were still a huge part of her life and she was not seeking any material benefit, this was just a voyage of personal discovery, nothing more than that.

'How do we know if she is your fucking daughter anyway?' said Sheila. 'Tell her we want a fucking DNA test. I'll give her a fucking voyage of discovery!'

'Now listen, Sheila!' I responded perhaps too sharply. 'Claire and I had a loving teenage sexual relationship, it's nothing to be ashamed of. It seems she became pregnant and because she comes from a Catholic family and we were so young, her parents sent her off to live with the nuns until the baby was born and adopted it out. That's what life was like then, don't you remember? Claire was a good person Sheila, she wouldn't tell Lisa a lie, I am not going to put Lisa through the trauma of a DNA test, to make her prove she is my daughter nor will I disrespect Claire by refusing to accept her word. For goodness sake I owe Claire an apology not a slap in the face, it must have been awful for her. Anyway Sheila,' I continued, 'none of this is bad news, this is good news. We don't live in the small-minded morality of that time anymore, let's embrace Lisa as good news.

Our world will be enriched and bigger for having her in it. This is not bad news'

'Oh for fuck's sake Harry, grow up,' said Sheila. 'She is after money, this is about inheritance, you never fucking understand people do you? We will talk about it when I get home.'

So, Sheila's position was clear, but so was mine. I was quite unmoved by her words and really did feel a connection with Lisa already. I was not going to let it go. As I put the mobile phone in my pocket I looked around me. I was quite alone in the empty industrial site. The crew, crane, trucks, equipment had all gone. I had been so absorbed in the two conversations that I hadn't noticed.

The very next day I wrote to Lisa and because talk is often cheap I enclosed an open return airline ticket for her from Auckland to Sydney to reinforce the sincerity of my invitation for her to visit.

Over the next couple of months we exchanged letters and phone calls. Then Lisa decided to accept my invitation to visit and we set dates for a long weekend together. Sheila was incandescent with rage when I told her. Although I was unsettled by her behaviour, I was quite determined and when at last she understood that she could not prevent the visit, she announced rules including but by no means limited to the important ruling that Lisa and I must never be alone together. Sheila had to be included at all times in all conversations. 'For goodness sake Sheila this is my biological daughter, what do you think I would do with her by myself?' I asked incredulously.

'She is another fucking woman on my turf, that's who she is!' was Sheila's surly response.

When we met at the airport, Lisa was all that I could have hoped for. This was my daughter. I was ready not just to accept her but to love her. It happened the moment I hugged her, my

34

emotional life really did expand. During the weekend we did lots of activities together as a family including dining out at restaurants, a night at the opera, a harbour cruise, and then time at our waterfront home at North Arm Cove.

Sadly, Lisa didn't reciprocate my affection, and even worse, she didn't like me at all. I suppose she had developed a construct in her imagination of the type of person she needed me to be and I was a huge disappointment. It wasn't just me that she didn't take to, she didn't like Josaphine either.

'I should never have come!' she said tearfully on Sunday afternoon and retreated to her bedroom to weep. With perfect timing Sheila followed her in to comfort her in her misfortune at having found her biological father and sister to be shallow and superficial people that she had nothing in common with. Sheila reminded her that her adoptive parents were her real father and mother who cared for her and loved her, we were not just strangers we were strange strangers.

Sheila's words were a great comfort to Lisa and they bonded in a friendship born out of their shared discomfort of suffering our company. I mentioned to Josaphine some time later that it was a bit of a paradox that Lisa would form a friendship with the one person in the home that didn't want her in our lives. 'I don't know about paradox Daddy, more like the ultimate insult,' she replied sourly, obviously shaken and hurt by Lisa's lack of empathy and poor regard for us.

The next day we delivered Lisa to the airport for her trip home. She hugged Sheila warmly, thanking her for her understanding and support, and then haltingly she told me that she had achieved what she needed from the visit, we were not her family, she was going to stop searching for something that didn't exist, she hoped that we would exchange Christmas cards, that would be enough, and then she was gone.

35

Sheila sighed with contentment on the way home. 'Thank God that's over, I do hope you two aren't upset that she couldn't stand you?' she said as she giggled with delight.

'Oh well, I suppose I will have to remain an only child,' Josaphine responded wistfully. I passed no remark, not knowing how I was supposed to feel or respond to any of it.

Without including or even informing Sheila, I wrote to Lisa every week after her visit always enclosing some small token gift for her and/or her children, technically my grandchildren. All relationships require effort and I wasn't going to let the small matter of her rejection of me stand in the way of maintaining and deepening the relationship. It was a slow process, but within a few months we were again exchanging telephone calls with little snippets of information about what was happening in our lives and bit by bit our relationship was developing. Lisa assumed, incorrectly, that Sheila was part of this process and in due course, as the relationship warmed, she wrote us a normal letter with odds and ends of news of her life, her children, just normal everyday news. Sheila was literally shaking with rage when I arrived home to find her with the open letter in her hand.

'What sort of a idiot are you?' she shouted. 'I had it all sorted out but you couldn't fucking leave it alone could you? You have been writing to that woman behind my back haven't you?'

'Sheila, this isn't about you,' I said firmly. 'That woman as you call her happens to be my daughter and her children are my grandchildren. Do you get it Sheila? I am going to construct a relationship with her and my grandchildren, they are my family, it's the right and proper thing to do, do you understand?'

'She isn't your daughter, she is just the product of a fuck you had more than 30 years ago. Now you listen to me and I'll tell you how it's going to be. It's her or me, it's as simple as

36

that, you cut off contact with her right now, it's over, If you don't, you don't have a marriage and let me remind you in case you have forgotten, all you own in life is a yellow tractor, every other asset is in my name, you don't have a house, you don't have a business, you are fucked without me, fucked! Do you understand that?'

She was right, of course, that was the way we had arranged our personal affairs. Sheila didn't hold any formal or informal executive position in any of our companies and I didn't own person assets in my name. It was basic commercial risk management based on total trust within the marriage and I had trusted Sheila, whatever faults she may have had. We were tight with one another on financial security but now the rules had changed.

I spent that night in a hotel. I didn't intend leaving her, but I couldn't find a set of words to take us forward. Apart from not being able to afford to leave Sheila, we were husband and wife in a secure marriage and had long since passed the point of trying to change each other. Although I was committed to my marriage, I knew that I couldn't and wouldn't give up Lisa. All I could do was buy some time until I could find a way to make it all work. I returned home from the hotel the next morning and mumbled my way through a reconciliation of sorts with Sheila. The next day I telephoned Lisa and requested that Sheila be dropped from the information loop until such time as I resolved some outstanding issues Sheila had with the relationship. I had brought myself some time but I was very aware that nothing had been resolved, it was another time bomb ticking in my life, waiting to go off.

I decided at the earliest opportunity to accept an invitation from Lisa to visit her at her home to meet her husband and children. I visited her twice in early 2000, explaining each absence to Sheila as a business trip. They were wonderful visits that I felt enriched us all. I also took the time to develop a functional telephone and email relationship with Claire. In the early stages of our contact Claire was a little suspicious of my motives, vaguely wondering if I was attempting to reawaken the romantic relationship of our youth. When she satisfied herself that there was no hidden agenda, she laughingly told me that she was both relieved and a little disappointed. 'Gosh human emotions are complicated,' she sighed.

The third huge issue that exercised my mind greatly in the second half of 1999 and early 2000 was the renegotiation of an existing contract by one of the companies I was a director and shareholder with a highly volatile new manager of a major client.

My particular concern was the potential negative impact that a specific minor worker's compensation claim may have on the contract income. In the early 1990s, four separate companies, each with different trade specialties – mechanical, electrical, civil and instrumentation maintenance and upgrade services – were the primary contractors at a local paper mill.

Although each contracting company had its own core trade specialty, there was considerable overlap in bidding for work and no structured coordination between the contractors. At that time one of my companies was one of the contractors, primarily providing civil services, but also providing significant engineering services.

The four principals of these four separate companies formed a new single company Process Engineering Technologies Pty Ltd, drawing staff, equipment and skills from their four parent companies. The primary purpose of this company was to enter into an annual multi-discipline contract to provide all their maintenance needs in a single package at a fixed price.

Apart from each of the principals becoming directors of the new company, each of the directors had specific executive responsibilities for the delivery of our specific trade specialties. We, the directors, all had extensive commercial interests unrelated to Process Engineering Technologies Pty Ltd and the paper mill that required our time, so our line managers looked after most of the day to day management issues but we still seemed to have considerable involvement in the detail of this business.

Apart from the routine daily, weekly, monthly maintenance tasks we provided to the mill using our regular on-site staff, once a year for a two-week 'shutdown' period we hired more than a hundred extra staff for extensive, intense, extra maintenance and capital upgrade work using the extra staff while the paper machines were shut down providing unencumbered access for the entire period. The civil works were my specific responsibility, and always included extensive capital works outside the fixed price contract. It was the civil arm of the business that always seemed to expand most during these shutdowns.

In early 2000, my fellow directors and I were involved in lengthy and difficult contract negotiations with the new mill manager. Apart from the normal commercial pressure on us to provide more services at a lower contract price, we were also dealing with a highly volatile, abrasive and unstable personality. Of the four directors, I was a particular target for his angry outbursts. Some of it was personal, but much of it related to the fact that so many essential civil services fell outside the fixed price contract, thus involving extra cost.

Although he was unconcerned with our staff performing repairs and maintenance as part of the fixed price contract, he would become angry to see any new works, authorised by his own staff, being carried out at extra cost. During the latest round of negotiations I tried to keep a low profile, leaving most of the face-to-face contact with him to my fellow directors. They weren't having an easy time of it either as his price and service expectations were way outside commercial reality. He would often fly into an uncontrollable rage and they would have to retreat. It was an awfully difficult and anxious time for us, as millions of dollars of revenue were at stake plus the jobs of more than a hundred of our employees.

It was in this commercial environment in early 2000 that I received a telephone call from WorkCover, the workers' compensation body, and learned that a formal complaint had been laid against us by a subcontractor. One of the sole trader subcontractors, who was obliged by law to have his own workers compensation insurance, had been hired by us in a one-off arrangement for three 10-hour shifts during the October 1999 shutdown and he claimed to have injured his back due to our negligent supervision while working for us scraping paint off the inside of a tank wall as preparation for its repainting.

I had no knowledge of it so I arranged an appointment with the WorkCover Inspector and made some inquiries I contacted the supervisor on the job, Jim. He remembered the man and the job when I questioned him about it. He also remembered that the man had complained that he had accidentally slipped into a sludge pit at the base of the tank when working and injured his back. 'Did you fill in an accident report Jim?,' I asked hopefully.

'No boss, I didn't. I didn't believe him, the pit had been covered, none of the other men saw anything, he didn't seem injured and it was all a bit silly really. At the time I thought he just wanted an excuse to go out for a smoke,' Jim responded earnestly.

After speaking with Jim I asked our accounts clerk to provide me with details of the payment to the contractor. During that conversation I discovered that when the fellow presented his invoice and collected a cheque in full payment he had asked our accounts clerk for details of our workers compensation policy but since he was neither an employee nor injured he wasn't given those details. So now I understood. The contractor probably wanted to make a bogus injury claim, not uncommon in our industry and he probably didn't have insurance of his own as required by law, so he wanted to make a claim on our insurance, but in order to do so he would need to prove we injured him, thus he had made his formal complaint to WorkCover. It was all pretty clear that this was just another scam.

The WorkCover Inspector interviewed Jim and I independently of each other. He was almost satisfied by the explanation but asked if he could interview the three other men on that shift to confirm Jim's version of events. I explained that these men were casual employees or contractors hired on a one-off basis for that specific shutdown period but I would find their details and forward them to him. He helpfully indicated that he would only need telephone contact with them as he accepted Jim's version at face value. He said that for his records it would be best if he had confirmation. He admonished us both to ensure that in future all claims of injuries were recorded, no matter how implausible. If the man had been injured and his claims were correct it would have been a very serious matter indeed. First, there was the issue of perhaps an unsafe workplace, then failure to report an accident, failure to provide the man with details of our insurance – the list of troubles seemed endless. He made it very clear that if this man had a valid case we would be prosecuted. As his immediate supervisor, Jim would be liable to a fine of up to $5,000, I would be liable for a fine of up to $25,000 and the company would be liable for a fine of up to $250,000. What he didn't say, and didn't know, was that that sort of public prosecution for a serious safety breach would probably tip the new Mill Manager over the edge in contract negotiations, the relationship was already too fragile, and it just couldn't withstand that sort of baggage. I knew also that although I had managed this issue well up until now, I was not out of trouble yet and it could all still go horribly wrong. How right I was.

The first casual worker was easy to contact and easy to deal with. I explained the details and he confirmed Jim's version of events to me. I explained that I could not pay him any money for his time in talking to WorkCover, as that would be a corrupt practice, but I could pay him two hours' pay at $18 which came to $36, the same rate of pay as he had been paid during the shutdown. It was not serious money, just token compensation for his time and effort. He was more than happy with the arrangement.

The second casual worker was a different story. I couldn't contact him at the address listed and received a bit of a hostile reception when I called there. It was reasonably obvious that this worker had been operating under a false name and false tax file number. He was probably claiming an unemployment benefit from the government at the time he was working for us. Whatever the problem was, he had gone to ground, I was never going to find him so I gave up.

The third worker was a young boy who didn't speak English very well. During the time that he had worked for us, he and Jim had spoken to each other primarily in Arabic, it was probably the main reason he had been deployed in Jim's team. He lived with relatives who were not his parents in the Western Suburbs of Sydney and I arranged by telephone to visit them one evening. On the appointed evening, I arrived at the home and was invited to meet with the youth and his uncle in the lounge room as the females and children busied themselves in the kitchen. His uncle explained that he would be acting as both interpreter and advisor to the youth.

I went through all the details in painstaking detail, pausing each few sentences to allow the uncle to interpret my words into Arabic. I explained that the WorkCover inspector would need to talk to the young fellow on the telephone and perhaps the uncle may have to assist with any language problems. I also explained the payment offer of $36 for his time and trouble. The uncle and the youth then spoke to each other at length in Arabic until at last the uncle spoke to me in English. 'Okay,' he said, 'he will say what you need him to say but a fair price you must pay for his help is $6,000.'

'Perhaps you don't understand,' I responded. 'I don't want him to say anything untruthful. I can't and won't bribe him, he must tell the truth whatever it is.'

'The truth may be anything,' the uncle ventured philosophically. 'The truth may help you or hurt you, the truth can go either way.'

'Now listen to me,' I replied slowly. 'I will not bribe anyone nor will I ask anyone to say anything untruthful. The most I am willing to pay in this case is a full day's pay, eight hours at $18 was $114, that is all, anything more would be bribery.' In my next telephone conversation with the WorkCover inspector I gave him details of the first casual worker that he could contact by phone. I told him about the second fellow who had given a false name and tax file number and finally told him that I was still tracking down the third fellow. So again I had another time bomb ticking, a problem quarantined but not resolved.

Another big issue in 2000 started with a telephone call from another client. Colin was about 50 years old, a well turned out 'man of the world' sort of fellow. He was the Engineering

Manager of a large industrial manufacturing site in Sydney and we had done business together for many years providing various contracting services. We normally had an easy, warm friendly relationship so I was a little surprised when he asked me, with a sharp edge to his voice, to come to the site he managed immediately.

Amongst the hundreds of contracts we had completed over the years for his company some years ago, we had, under properly controlled conditions, removed asbestos pipes in a redundant section of a power plant on his site. The removed asbestos had been properly disposed of at an approved landfill tip and the steel pipes disposed of to a scrap metal merchant. It had at the time and in my memory been just been another job so I had no reason to think of it as I drove over to meet him.

When I arrived Colin met me in the car park with only the most cursory of greetings and asked me to take a long walk with him down to a storage yard at the rear of his site. Inside the yard he walked me around, behind some of his company's old mothballed machinery that had not been moved for years and there, unexpectedly were about 20 asbestos lagged steam pipes on the ground. The lagging was broken here and there with asbestos spilled out and blown this way and that. Several of the pipes had labels on them with my company logo with a warning to keep clear as this was highly dangerous asbestos. These pipes were obviously a batch from that removal job of several years ago.

I now clearly remembered that we had actually used the front half of that particular storage yard as a storage base during that job and our supervisor, who had earned a big bonus on that specific job, had terminated his employment with us shortly afterwards. It was now obvious that our supervisor had probably dumped the pipes there, out of sight and out of mind, in order to reduce costs on the job and increase his bonus based on cost minimisation. It was awful, dangerous and illegal as well as a huge mess.

Colin's face was white as he spoke with a choking voice. 'Can you imagine how this will play out if news of this gets out Harry? WorkCover will close this entire site until their investigation is completed. The unions and WorkCover representatives will wring their hands on the television news and talk about "cowboy contractors and inadequate supervision". Do you understand Harry? You are the cowboy contractor and I am the inadequate supervision. Neither of us will ever work in Sydney ever again, we will be fucked Harry, really fucked!'

'Who knows about it now?' I asked hopefully.

'Only me and a forklift driver who came into the yard this morning to drop off an old motor. He didn't know if it was asbestos or not. I looked at it with him and told him I would have it checked out by experts today. You are the expert and you have just told me that it isn't asbestos haven't you? Even though I have your assurance that it isn't asbestos, it is still a mess and I want you to clean it up. You need to come after dark tonight Harry, here is a key to the yard gate. I will tell security your company is collecting some old pipes from here tonight. You will need to be quick and clean. It needs to be spotless in the morning Harry, not a trace or we are both fucked.' His hand was shaking as he handed me the key.

I didn't dare use any of our own employees so I arranged with Pete, who was the owner operator of a large truck that had its own tray mounted Hiab crane, to do the job with me.

I did all the dirty work myself, leaving Pete on the crane controls. I wrapped each pipe with plastic, sealing the flap with duct tape. Then as Pete lifted them each slightly off the ground with his crane, I sealed the ends before they were loaded onto the truck. It took four hours to complete this operation, with all the pipes on the truck and the load covered with a tarpaulin. It then took me another two hours to scrape, sweep and bag up all the loose asbestos that had spilled in the yard. After I had finished, I lifted a drain grate in the corner of the yard and stood in the sump. Pete ran a hose over me as I stripped off my coveralls, then inner clothing, then finally my protective breathing mask.

Shivering with cold I bagged up all the clothing and mask for disposal while still naked, then had Pete run the hose over me again before I dried myself and dressed myself in a clean pair of disposable overalls. Despite the fact that Pete had been well clear of the dirty work, I repeated the same clean off process with him. We had both been wearing protective clothing and breathing masks for more than six hours so we hadn't spoken to one another or stopped for a break until then and we were both dead on our feet. 'You could have told me I had to throw away my clothes. They were a brand new pair of jeans,' was the first words Pete said to me.

'Add it to the bill Pete,' was my weary response.

As any asbestos disposed of at the tip has to come from a registered asbestos removal job I couldn't get rid of the load immediately. It had to stay on the truck for another week until I could combine it with another asbestos disposal load going to the tip from one of our current jobs that did have registration. It had cost me a night's work, $10,000 to Pete, but at last it was gone, into an authorised landfill tip. It was a huge relief but sadly that wasn't the end of it. Although it had not changed the contract price of the current job, I added it to the landfill tip from my German client. He noticed receipt of 23 tonnes and knew it didn't tally with his small 3- to 4-tonne job. When he queried it with me, I explained that I had just added some extra waste asbestos to his job for the purpose of tipping, it didn't change the price to him at all. 'No, no, no, Harry this is not suitable at all.' He informed me in his crisp German accent, we want a correct paperwork trail for any asbestos disposal, saying 'the legislation is very clear. You must arrange to amend the paperwork to separate out our waste from the other job.'

'Sure,' I replied. 'I will arrange that, no problem but it may take a little while for me to work through the bureaucratic process with the landfill people so why don't I delay invoicing you for this work until I have fixed it up to give me an incentive to hurry.'

'Excellent Harry,' he positively beamed at me with absolutely no understanding of what I would need to do to fix it. As I drove away from his office I tried to figure out how I could fix it. 'Oh Jesus, where will this end,' I groaned out loud. 'Am I really going to create fraudulent paperwork to cover this up. What a mess, another mess.'

It is important to place these problems in context. My normal commercial life, filled with normal levels of success and failure, continued at breakneck speed requiring my constant time, energy, intelligence and ingenuity. I was well suited to that type of normal, high pressure commercial life. But the growing list of problems was something different. I realised clearly that I was unable to survive commercially in my current form and, worse, if I didn't take action at least some of my problems would overflow onto the companies I held directorships and minority shareholdings in. If I didn't take decisive action soon before some of the problems started to unravel, I would damage the commercial interests of my business partners as well as myself. I felt I had a duty to act immediately and decisively.

At the first opportunity, I announced to my business partners, staff and clients that although I intended to retain my shareholdings and directorships, I would be retiring from all my executive positions and duties within the companies in 90 days time. I indicated that after my resignation took effect, I intended to spend a lot of my personal time working on a personal development project with Aboriginal people in western NSW that I already had some minor involvement with.

Although I had fully discussed the problems with Sheila, she was incredulous when I made the announcement. 'Are you out of your mind?!' she said. 'You needn't think I am leaving Sydney to spend time in the desert. You can do that by yourself.'

'Sheila, you must understand, things can't stay the same. The commercial boat we are on is sinking, its time to gather our valuables and get into our lifeboat,' I said. 'It's either that or drown.'

This is what has to happen. First I had to resign from all my executive positions and leave town so that I am not easily accessible to answer questions. Anybody who knows me will know that I am out of business and involved in some vague charity work out west. That will almost certainly solve four of the problems, I won't be around and they will probably just die a natural death.

Secondly sooner or later we had to deal with the Ukrainians. At some time, we had to settle on a price and pay them to end it. Once they knew I was withdrawing from commercial life, I was hoping that the final price we had to pay would reduce. I just wouldn't have the commercial value and they will know that. Slowly but surely over the next year or so we could sell up our interests then buy a motel or hotel on the north coast, enough income but no real stress. I didn't, at that stage, discuss the unresolved issue of my relationship with Lisa but believed it too could be worked out with time, goodwill and compromise.

'I'm not going to any Aboriginal camp in the desert,' she

said. 'You run off and hide but I'm not going anywhere and I'm not paying any of my money to some blackmailing Ukrainians. Why don't you face it all like a man!'

And so it went on between us but I felt confident I had taken the first critical steps to protect us. I had resigned from my executive positions and in 90 days I would make myself extremely difficult to contact. I had taken out life insurance to protect Sheila and Josaphine in case the worst happened between now and settlement with the Ukrainians. At this time we increased the life insurance payout to $3.5 million.

Now all I could do was lower my profile and keep all the balls in the air until Sheila and I reached agreement on a pathway forward. By late May, our relationship improved considerably and I felt more confident that we could resolve our differences. As she was leaving for Egypt on the first leg of a world trip with her sister, I had a final conversation with Sheila about the issues.

'Listen, this can probably all wait until your return,' I started. 'But if the Ukranian thing turns ugly, I may have to just disappear to survive, so for goodness sake don't think I have run off with a floozy if I am not here when you get back. I will turn up and it will be all right.' She gave her new breasts a jiggle and cheerfully responded. 'Ha, how could you ever give up this body?'

Apart from her weight, Sheila always took exceptional care with skin care, hair, clothing and presentation in general. Despite all of her care, age was having a very normal effect on how she looked. She tried to stem the tide and by 1999 she had a new set of fashionably large breasts fitted, seemingly endless surgery on her face, and teeth work, but none of it satisfied her.

3

Surprising Sheila

AUGUST 2000

From my flat in Kensington, I decided I had to meet Sheila to discuss the situation and find a way forward. Although I was apprehensive about how her initial reception would be, I was desperate, heartsick and lonely. In an almost childlike way I wanted and needed to be cuddled. Despite all Sheila's faults, my faults and our imperfect marriage, I believed that we both loved each other and were committed to each other as a couple. Sheila also was my only link with reality. My current life was imaginary, but insufficiently imagined. I used a false name and had some money, but I didn't have a driver's licence or a Medicare card, passport or any other identity document. I just didn't exist.

The full enormity of my situation weighed heavily on me and I felt sick knowing that I would never ever see my siblings, my daughter, Lisa, grandchildren, family and friends ever again. I felt confident that in time Josaphine would find a way back into my life, but who knew how long that would take or what the circumstances may be. I felt isolated and lonely.

We lived in a very nice three-bedroom terrace home with a rear yard and off-street parking in Waterloo Street in Sydney. We were more than a little pleased with its location; it is about as close to downtown Sydney as one can live in a proper house instead of an apartment. As the street was predominantly commercial, we had very little to do with our neighbours. Across the street from our home was the large multistorey Readers Digest Building, to our left were a few other domestic terrace houses and to our right was a specialist brothel, The Fat Lady Fetish, that, as the name suggests, offered the services of very plump ladies to men who had that particular sexual interest. Although we were on nodding terms with some of the large ladies who worked there, for obvious reasons we did not linger for casual conversation when our paths crossed. The short lane that provided access to the rear yards to both our home and The Fat Lady Fetish had three tiny houses without any front yards, their front doors opening onto the laneway itself. Over the years, I often saw furtive men scurrying to and from the discreet rear entry of The Fat Lady Fetish. I had a handful of passing encounters with one or other of the tenants entering or leaving one of their little laneway houses but no real contact, so we would never have recognised each other by sight. In preparing to meet with Sheila I had no hesitation or trepidation about walking up the dark rear lane, late at night, unlocking the rear gate then walking into our rear yard and that is exactly what I did to meet with Sheila. I was aware there was a very real danger that Sheila may mistake me for a burglar or worse if I just walked in on her so I decided to leave a note on the kitchen bench next to the electric kettle, where I knew she would make herself a cup of coffee first thing in the morning.

The note said: 'Don't be afraid, I am alive, waiting in the laundry. Love Harry.'

Her face was white and her hands were shaking violently when she opened the laundry door with the note still in her hand. I smiled reassuringly and held my arms open ready to embrace her but it wasn't going to be like that.

'How could you do this?' she opened the conversation. 'I thought you were dead, Have you any idea what I have been through?'

We didn't embrace. She folded her arms just below her large artificial breasts and listened as I talked. I reminded her that we had discussed the option of me disappearing.

'I didn't think for one minute that you would go through with it! What sort of a fuckwit are you anyway?'

The conversation went back and forwards for about an hour, never making any progress on a way forward, just rehashing how it had come to this and how I could have handled it differently. Then all of a sudden she became aware that she was having a conversation with a person who was supposed to be dead and my very presence placed her at risk. 'You can't stay here!,' she said, 'Imagine if someone hears us or sees you. What were you thinking?'

After another brief and heated discussion we agreed that there was a significant risk that I would be recognised if I left in daylight hours so it would be much better for me to wait until nightfall and leave in the dark. Sheila wanted to get out and about with her normal routine for the day and wanted me to stay in the laundry until after dark. I insisted on coming into my own home but did consent to her request not to talk or move about in the house. We also reached agreement on a time and place, away from home, for our next meeting to continue our discussions on what the long-term options were. Sheila ushered me into the bedroom, we embraced awkwardly without kissing, then she was gone.

After she left I realised that the meeting had gone much worse that I had expected and our future together as a couple now was by no means certain. I had anticipated her anger and expected her to be unreasonable, but her emotional disconnection from me was unexpected and alarming. It was very clear that she had blocked out most memories of the conversations we had about all the problems and options prior to my disappearance. She wordlessly delivered two sandwiches and a cup of coffee to me a little after two o'clock that afternoon and then again at 6.30pm. Apart from those brief appearances, I was quite alone. At about 7.30pm she came into the bedroom and turned on the small bedside television with the volume turned up loud allowing us to have a brief whispered conversation about when I would leave and confirming arrangements for our next meeting. Prior to the meeting I had imagined that after her initial anger subsided we would kiss, cuddle and perhaps make love, but we were obviously too distant from one another to even cuddle. Because her level of anxiety was so high I left sooner rather than later, walking down the laneway a little before 9.00pm.

I was very aware that my entire existence, not just my welfare, was in Sheila's hands. When I had started this journey I didn't doubt Sheila's loyalty for one moment. I knew she could be difficult and at times downright nasty but I had never doubted she would stand by me. I had imagined that we had many years together and had been through too much as a couple for our marriage to end. I now felt uncertain and very insecure.

We had arranged for our next meeting to take place in the rear of our campervan, with the curtains drawn, parked in a shopping centre car park. She arrived almost on time and settled down onto the couch seat next to me. Although our relationship was by no means at the kiss and cuddle stage, it was clear that the initial shock had passed and her attitude was warmer and softer than it had been at our first meeting. I held both her hands and told her how good she looked, how much I missed her and loved her. I reminded her that we had been together for more than 25 years through good times and bad, that we could weather this storm together if we both remained strong and committed to our marriage. I spoke solidly for more than an hour, outlining my understanding of where we had been. I took ownership of the problems that had brought us to this point, accepting that at times I had allowed my personal greed and ego to override sound commercial governance. I accepted responsibility for the situation and apologised.

I said that I believed that because my body had not been found, although there would be general acceptance that I had probably drowned, the coroner would probably make an open finding with no death certificate for at least seven years. 'A lot can happen in seven years Sheila. The problems we are now facing will be long gone by then, I will be yesterday's man if anyone remembers me at all. Let's face it, there is no prospect of the life insurance being paid out so AMP won't care, there are no real legal issues of concern, we don't owe anyone any money, none of the companies we have shares in are in any sort of trouble, our real estate was all mortgage free, nobody will really care one way or other what really happened to me.'

I suggested that in a few months, as soon as interest died down, Sheila should start to liquidate all of our assets so that within 12 to 18 months we would be cashed up. During this period I suggested that I could remain nearby and meet frequently with Sheila to give her business advice. We could spend little holidays together, a few days at a time, to keep our romantic, emotional and commercial connection current.

When we were all cashed up, we could slip out of town together and buy a motel in country Queensland. Sheila could break off most of her connections but still visit her mother and other members of her family a couple of times a year. People would soon lose interest in us. Josaphine's loyalty to the family unit was beyond doubt so once we relocated she could come and go as she pleased.

'I know this isn't a great plan,' I said 'But we haven't really broken any laws. We will be safe and can stay together as a family. We can and will review our situation and our options from time to time. The world, our place in it and how we view it, will be very different in a few years time won't it?'

Sheila gave me a courteous if unenthusiastic hearing. I was grateful to her for that and thankful also that it was obvious from her feedback that she had a much clearer recollection of our discussions prior to my disappearance. She did, however, have a very different opinion to me on the best way forward. 'You need to contact the police Harry. Tell them that you had a mental breakdown because of all the mental stress, tell them that's why you did it. It happens all the time, you won't get into any trouble,' she told me earnestly.

'That's great Sheila,' I responded. 'The police aren't in the business of helping people. They never were and they never will be in that business. It is their job to enforce the law, arresting people then to appear on television to show that the taxpayers are getting value for money. Their input will not just inflame the danger I am in, it would completely ruin my reputation. If I did survive their involvement, most of my clients, business partners and suppliers won't want to do business with me on my return because I will be labelled as unstable. I know that doesn't matter in the long run anymore, but doing it that way will immediately put me at risk and devalue our commercial interests. Far more important than my personal reputation, no matter if people think I am crazy or not, is that we still haven't worked out how to handle the issues, what to really do about Alek and his associates, what to do about Lisa, what to do about the blackmailer in the workers' compensation claim, the asbestos problem, etcetera, etcetera. Sheila I would love to return. I miss being me more than you can ever know, it has been gut wrenchingly awful for me to loose my identity, but at the moment we are no further ahead, we must resolve these matters before I can come back, if I am ever come back.'

'Harry, you are such a drama queen,' she said with impatience. 'Just tell the police about Alek, let them deal with it. As for little Lisa, well, she is out of our life now so she is not an issue. As far as you need to give evidence in the workers' compensation thing, just tell the guy if he threatens to blackmail you we will report him to the police and he will go to jail, I guarantee it. None of this stuff is any big deal. You have been through much worse than this before. You just need to toughen up and face it. You can handle it, you always have.'

'I don't think you are right,' I replied cautiously. 'I may not be correct. Perhaps I have got some of it out of proportion. I am willing to take that on board but nobody is threatening to kill you Sheila. Perhaps you would feel differently in my place.'

At long last, although we didn't have agreement and there were huge differences in our positions, we were at last having a real conversation about the real issues, those things that really mattered. The conversation continued for another two hours then we had to suspend it because our allocated time for the meeting had elapsed and we agreed that it was sound risk management for Sheila not to be missing for large periods of time. We held a follow-up meeting in a different car park the following week with the discussion continuing where we had left off. We were unable to agree on our future direction, but at long last Sheila seemed to grasp the gravity of my situation. She began to explore another option.

'Harry, if you can't return to normal life you need to leave Australia, it's madness for you to stay here. It's only a matter of time until you are recognised. You need to wear different sort of clothes, grow a beard, you need to change who you are and leave the country.'

'How on earth do you think I can travel overseas?' I asked. 'My passport must be invalid, I am a dead person, I don't exist anymore.'

'You need to buy a new identity and password from the underworld,' she said earnestly.

'The underworld! Are you for real?' I spluttered. 'How on earth do I contact the underworld. Shall I look under U in the yellow pages for underworld or under C for criminals. For God's sake Sheila I don't know how to contact the underworld and I don't want to know.'

'Don't be so stupid' she replied angrily. 'Surely you can find out how to make contact with them. I don't know how to do it either but I do know you can't stay here in Australia.'

'Maybe you're right.' I mused. 'Perhaps a new start in a different country would be best, I just hadn't considered it, that's all. I suppose I could sail a yacht from Darwin at the top of Australia to Indonesia, it's not that far, I could do that and arrive using my own passport. The Indonesian immigration system won't know I am dead, I can't imagine it is linked to the Australian system. They will just accept my passport at face value. If you meet me there we can fly out to another country and start again. That's a viable option for me but can you do it Sheila? If we move interstate here in Australia you can telephone and visit your family, particularly your mother on a regular basis but if we move overseas you won't be able to return regularly and in fact you may never see them again.'

'I will have to think about that,' she replied thoughtfully. 'I really don't want to spend the rest of my life looking over my shoulder but I can't see any other realistic option. You can't stay here in Australia, it's as simple as that.'

As we started to explore this option together some warmth returned to our relationship, we kissed awkwardly, told each other that we still loved each other and a great deal of the tension between us seemed to wash away. After discussing the strain the current situation was placing on our marriage, we agreed to postpone making any long-term decisions on our future until we had re-established the emotional and physical bonds of our relationship. To that end I invited her to come and spend a two or three week holiday with me in the Kensington flat I had rented but she turned me down on the basis that she felt unable to be absent from family and friends. This seemed a little disingenuous as she was often went away on little holidays during our marriage but perhaps her level of contact with them had changed now that she was officially a widow.

As an alternative to her visiting me we considered the option of me visiting her at our city house in Waterloo Street. We agreed that the risk was reasonable if I limited my movement within the home and we restricted our conversation to the bedroom when the television was on to mask our voices. The following night, using the same routine as my first visit, just after 10 o'clock I walked up the lane, into our rear yard then into our home. Within an hour we were in bed making love and an hour later we were sitting naked on the bed, sipping champagne and talking in whispers.

During the following two weeks Sheila continued her routine, including telephone calls to family and friends, shopping trips and visitors coming and going from the home. I spent most of my daytime hours in the bedroom reading and watching television. In the evenings, when she had no visitors, we ate dinner together downstairs in the dining room before going to bed early, like a honeymoon couple to make love again. Sheila was more than a little pleased with the way her new, surgically enhanced breasts looked and enjoyed showing them off. After making love we would often sit naked, cross-legged in the middle of the bed together, sipping champagne and eating strawberries out of a bowl between us. I had hoped that we would really get close again and bond as a couple but it wasn't really to be. I felt that Sheila was really just having sex with me more than making love. She was more physical and enthusiastic than she had ever been and during and after orgasm she had taken to saying 'Oh, fuck, that's good!' but with no hint of an 'I love you.'

It wasn't just our sex life that had changed. The power dynamics within our entire relationship had really shifted. She was now in charge of everything, there was no balance at all. We discussed family, our relationship and without pressing too hard I tried to learn what was happening with our various commercial interests. Sheila had appointed a trusted former direct employee, who now worked as the inhouse accountant with a large company we still had a shareholding in, as her representative, to deal with the various companies we still had interests in.

She had developed a routine of having a two-hour meeting with him once every week to sign any documents and cheques that he needed. Very little of commercial substance was discussed at these meetings. She became very hostile towards me when I asked her to get specific accounting details from him relating to the financial performance and status of the various companies we were involved with.

'Don't be so stupid!,' she would say. 'He knows that I don't understand that stuff!'

I retreated but resolved that when my visit with her ended and I again had access to a computer, I would type up a simple checklist on each of the companies, questions it would not be unreasonable for her to ask. For example, how much money or overdraft each company had in the bank at the last day of each month, how much they were owed by debtors on that day and how much they owed to creditors. Simple home economics bookkeeping – surely those were questions she could feel comfortable asking. In the meantime I had no idea what was happening to our commercial interests.

During this time with Sheila I learned that my passport and driver's licence had been given to our family solicitor as part of his preparation for a coroner's court hearing. It was unclear if they had now been passed on to the police. For me to move about and re-establish my identity in another country I needed that passport back.

Sheila and I discussed the forthcoming inquest at length and surprisingly agreed about the outcome. Due to the absence of a body it was almost certain that the coroner would declare an open finding and highly improbable that a death certificate would be issued earlier than five years, probably seven, perhaps 10 years from now. Sheila was becoming increasingly enthusiastic about me sailing out to Indonesia. We both agreed that we would need to wait until after the inquest before attempting to recover the passport from the solicitor. Sheila saw no reason for me to delay my departure. 'You can live on the yacht in Indonesia much cheaper than you can live here,' she suggested. 'Perhaps you may even find a temporary job there?'

Whenever I raised the matter of selling our assets and details of her meeting me in Indonesia she became hostile. 'I will know when the time is right,' she insisted. 'I have always had an instinct for trouble and timing that you have always lacked!'

My time with Sheila was drawing to a close and at a superficial level it had been a success. We had shared the memories of many years together, we slept together in the same bed, had sex almost every night, sometimes twice a night. There was a loose agreement that I would sail to Indonesia, and when the time was right Sheila would sell our assets and join me there. From there we would fly out to a third country to settle, probably Spain. Underneath that success, however, I had some deep concerns. In reality our sex life had been just that, sex without any real demonstration of love. There didn't seem to be any emotional depth to the physical. On commercial issues Sheila treated my interests as unwelcome, an intrusion on her business. Whenever I raised the subject of selling our assets she was nasty. It was clear that we still had a considerable distance to travel in the reconciliation process and I probably had to accept that the power dynamics in our relationship had changed forever.

Before my departure we agreed that I would return for a weekend sleepover in one month and a month after that we would spend two weeks together at our country home in North Arm Cove. The night of my departure Sheila was in a state of high anxiety about the risk that I might be seen as I was leaving. We didn't make love, the farewell embrace and kiss was awkward, then a little before midnight I stepped out into the rear lane and left the way I had come in. I walked up the hill and over to Anzac Parade where I caught a bus back to my little flat in Kensington. All was quiet as I let myself in, sat down, very alone and opened a bottle of champagne. With a steady stream of tears running down my face, I drank the whole bottle, then without pausing I opened another. In my mind I reviewed all that I had learned in the last two weeks with deep sadness.

It was very clear that it would have been more convenient for everyone if I really had drowned that night. Sheila informed me that our daughter Josaphine was overseas, visiting her man friend in the Isle of Wight, getting on with her life. Lisa, she told me, had accepted my death without any real concern. The reaction of my eldest sibling True was the biggest surprise. I was confident that she would understand that I wasn't dead, she knew me well enough to know on face value it was deeply implausible. Sheila had told me that not only had True accepted the news at face value, she was now developing a deep sisterly relationship with Sheila. She telephoned Sheila on a regular basis and was now encouraging Sheila to start a romantic life, to enjoy her social and sexual freedom. Their friendship seemed incredible. Sheila had never liked any of my siblings and had always had particular disdain for True – now they were friends. I was more than just disappointed, perhaps unrealistically, I was scandalised that True was encouraging Sheila to explore a romantic life. 'Even if she does believe I am dead, it has only been a few months. Gosh my body is hardly cold in the ground!' I muttered out loud as I slipped away in to an inebriated slumber.

I woke up the following morning more than a little hung over from too much champagne and far, far too much self pity. 'This journey was never for the faint hearted, you do understand that don't you,' I told myself. 'You can still do this, but to use Sheila's words, you really will need to stiffen up.' So it was with firm resolve that I cleaned myself up and put on a fresh positive attitude.

I returned to my daily routine of swimming laps each morning before visiting the library and art gallery each day but my intellectual focus had shifted. I now spent a great deal of time thinking about the details of our commercial and personal interests that would need attention before we could move onto then next phase. I allocated time each afternoon to preparing notes on actions Sheila needed to take and the commercial questions she needed to ask her advisors at their meeting. I redrafted it several times, editing out technical details to make it as simple as possible until I felt she had a documented plan she would be comfortable with. I posted it off to her, hoping she would have an open mind when she received them.

One month after my last visit, on a Friday night at the agreed time, I walked up the rear lane and into our Waterloo Street home for my scheduled weekend sleepover with Sheila. We had sex together on both Friday and Saturday nights but it wasn't making love, we weren't close at all and I felt even more isolated and lonely each time. I tried to discuss the document I had posted to her but she didn't want to discuss it at all, in fact she didn't want to discuss commercial issues at all.

'Listen, just stay out of my business will you,' she said. 'You are not involved and don't understand the way I work.' She now regarded the business interests as her personal domain and I was an unwelcome intruder. It was clear also that although she was going to use some of the notes I had prepared for her, most of it would be discarded. She spent most of the daytime periods of that weekend away from me, either out and about at the shops or downstairs in the rear yard smoking cigarettes. Her anger was always just below the surface, waiting to bubble up so I took great care not to pressure her to follow any of the directions I had given her in my notes. 'They are just suggestions,' I told her. 'You are the person dealing with the issues so, of course you must do whatever you feel is best, I am just trying to help.'

I told myself privately to let it all go. It doesn't really matter what happens to our business interests, the important tasks were to save our marriage, our real estate and our savings so that we could make a fresh start again together. The weekend ended and we parted with an awkward embrace. I could feel her relief as I walked out the gate. This time when I returned to my Kensington flat, despite the hurt, I went to bed without tears or champagne. Clearly I had stiffened up.

One month later, as arranged, I walked into the rear yard of our city home ready to travel to North Arm Cove. It was much earlier this time, just after dark and I waited in the outside laundry next to the yard. Almost immediately Sheila came out and opened the rear door of our family car, parked in the yard. I quickly and wordlessly slid into the car and lay down on the back seat covering myself with a blanket Sheila had left for me. The car was already loaded with minor provisions for our holiday together so without further delay Sheila drove out of the gate within minutes of my arrival. When we reached the northern freeway I pulled off the blankets and climbed into the front seat next to Sheila. Away from Sydney, Sheila seemed more relaxed and was brimming over with excitement at the news that our daughter Josaphine was pregnant, we were going to be grandparents together. It was a carefree trip, setting the mood for the entire holiday. We sang along to songs on the radio and laughed about becoming grandparents, it was a very happy time for us. It was wonderful to be in 'Toad Hall', our country home, again. We laughed, had a lot of sex and ate too much as we drank wine with the sounds of waves breaking on our sea wall just 30 metres from the open balcony sliding doors. It was all so relaxing. One important difference between Toad Hall and our Sydney home is that Sheila felt able to smoke cigarettes inside without having too much effect on the air inside. The rooms in Toad Hall are much bigger than the city terrace, with the main lounge room being almost 40 square metres and glass sliding doors opening onto the sea breeze. Although this may seem a small thing it meant that Sheila didn't have to take a cigarette break outside every half hour or so and it certainly improved her mood. It was in this relaxed atmosphere, lounging on the couch together, looking out on the harbour that Sheila raised the subject of my proposed yacht trip out of Darwin to Indonesia and we discussed the various factors that would influence timing.

I explained to Sheila that, as a matter of economy, I would need to buy an inexpensive, older yacht without a lot of automated equipment. Although I am a very experienced harbour sailor, I had very little experience of sailing and navigating offshore by myself so it was vital that I didn't sail during the tropical hurricane season. 'I just don't have the experience and skills to take an old yacht I don't know through a big storm,' I told her. 'I could drown!' We both laughed at the irony.

We both agreed that although Sheila would start selling assets at that time it was not necessary for the sales process to be completed before my departure. Sheila was right when she said that I could live inexpensively on the yacht in Indonesia, giving her time to complete the process in an orderly manner before joining me for the next phase.

The next issue was my passport. Although, of course, I intended to depart from Australia without clearing customs and immigration it would be helpful to have it on me when I arrived in Indonesia. I may have been able to just slip in but if an Indonesian immigration official spotted the boat I would be asked to produce my passport. I certainly couldn't leave Indonesia without a passport. I knew that my passport was still being held by our family solicitor, awaiting the coronial inquest into my disappearance, expected to be held around April or March in 2001.

Sheila felt she would have to wait a month or two after the inquest before asking for my passport and other documents to be returned to her without arousing suspicion. That timing fitted perfectly with my yacht voyage, anytime between April and July would be the perfect time for me to sail.

Another factor was the unexpected news that Josaphine was going to have a baby in March. I was, of course, very eager to meet with Josaphine but understood that there could be legal implications for her in the future about meeting me before the inquest. We agreed that I should delay meeting with Josaphine and our new grandchild until sometime in April, after the inquest and, of course. It was now becoming more and more probable that I would leave Australia on or about June 2001, one full year after my disappearance. At last we seemed to be pulling in the same direction together as a couple. It was true that I still had to be careful not to interfere or even ask too many questions about Sheila's management of our commercial and personal interests, the power dynamics of our relationship had shifted but I accepted all that, I really had let it all go.

It was very clear to me that Sheila found my visits to our Waterloo Street home very stressful so we agreed to limit them to two brief scheduled sleepover visits before April. We agreed that in April we would have a family holiday together at Toad Hall with Josaphine and our new grandchild. Apart from having a happy, loving holiday I considered the real success of our time together was our success in reaching agreement about our future direction. We drove back to Sydney in the darkness of early evening and all too soon it was time for me to step out of the car in a Sydney shopping centre car park, back into my solitary life again.

I no longer felt so alone, this was just time that had to pass until Sheila and I could start together again overseas as a couple. I was really looking forward to reconnecting with Josaphine. I didn't know how the father of her baby fitted into her life, or what the dynamics of that relationship were, but I felt confident that after our meeting we would all find a process for us to share family time together again on a reasonably regular basis, somehow that would work itself out.

I also now stopped worrying about what was happening to our commercial interests. They were I knew, still providing Sheila with a substantial monthly income. In due course, when the time came for Sheila to start selling assets the shares in particular may well be worth far less than when I disappeared. If she secured good prices I would consider it a bonus but it really didn't matter as our real estate and cash would be more than enough to give us a fresh start. Another big change in my daily life was the time I spent at creative writing each day at the library; it was time to face the ugly truth that I would never be a poet and I would never develop as a poet so it was time to give it up. I spent my creative writing time on short stories of about 2000 words instead, they were essays really. I worked on three at any given time, developing those in which I detected promise and discarding those where it was absent.

I had also changed my vehicle. The campervan was really unsuitable in the city and I was always fearful of a minor traffic accident due to the poor driver's visibility – that would have turned into a disaster given the fact that I wasn't alive. I bought an old Volvo sedan that was more suited to my needs and safer in traffic. I also started to think about my planned yacht voyage from Australia to Indonesia. I bought and studied nautical maps covering the area from Darwin to Singapore. I had no geographical experience in that area at all and the more I studied, the more I became aware of the hazards. It was more than a little daunting to be taking the journey by myself.

The next sleepover visit with Sheila, as arranged, was brief and thankfully uneventful. I arrived just before dawn on

Saturday morning and departed just after 10 on Sunday night. We really only spent Saturday night together. Sheila was still very anxious but tried harder to maintain an even temper and I was more understanding of her needs and fears. It was another successful meeting on several levels and I felt quite reassured when I returned to my little flat in Kensington. I was starting to feel safe again.

The six-month lease on the Kensington flat was due to expire in early February and although it had served me well, I decided to move rather than renew it. Kensington had never been a wise location for me to live, it was far too close to my former life with lots of people who knew me living nearby. Rather than rent another flat, I decided to take a room in one of the many inexpensive private hotels that were always advertising vacancies. I discovered that I didn't need anything more than a room – I never entertained at home, it was really just a place for me to sleep and write.

I was also keen to change from a fixed term lease of a flat to the week by week arrangement that a private hotel allowed, so I could leave quickly without too much fuss or cost whenever it suited me. After inspecting several private hotels I finally selected a hotel right in the heart of the seaside suburb of Manly.

The building was a huge, rambling and rundown, probably a grand seaside resort hotel from the 1920s that now looked like a haunted house from a movie set. I selected it despite its appearance due to its excellent location near the main seaside promenade, allowing me to walk to the beach in minutes. The shopping centre, hotels, cafés, internet cafés etc. were all just minutes away and it was just 10 minutes' walk from the Manly ferry terminal allowing me access to downtown Sydney, the library, the art gallery and the botanical gardens – all very important in my life. It was in fact the perfect location for my needs at that time.

When I moved in, still as Bill Teare, I discovered that although my room was clean and functional, the common areas, hallways, dining area and toilet facilities were even more rundown than the exterior. Beneath the ravaged exterior was an undeniable elegance, a sort of crumbling grandeur that I found quite endearing. This grand old building would have been a worthwhile restoration project if it had been started 20 years earlier, but now sadly it was too late. The ancient dining room was open five nights a week with affordable, plain evening meals available on a pay as you go basis. About 25 of the 60 odd hotel guests dined there several nights a week and during the time I lived there I formed a slight acquaintance with many of them as we often shared dining tables. There were five middle aged country women who had all run away from their respective husbands and families in country towns, each starting a new anonymous life in the big city. Four retired, elderly men had for one reason or other cut the ties with their families and was living out their twilight years there. Many of the others seemed to be a mix of different sorts of misfits who, for a variety of reasons, had fallen on hard times. Having found themselves broke and alone most were trying to restart their lives. I introduced myself as an unsuccessful author who was trying to write and live on a modest income. This explanation, which seemed at the time to be very close to the truth, was accepted by the other guests without question. We each had an individual story but the common thread was our social isolation and reduced circumstances. I couldn't have found a better place to live or more suitable people to live with in Sydney; it was perfect and fitted me like a glove.

I settled into my new life with a slightly changed daily routine.

Most mornings I took a brisk five kilometre walk along the Manly seaside promenade. I walked among a delightful community of regulars along the same route as me for their daily exercise. The wide sweeping beach with its glistening ocean, sometimes with wild pounding waves was in sharp contrast with the modern, busy resort town on the other side of the road yet they seemed to belong together. The whole scene was invigorating. After my walk I would often have coffee and toast at one of the local cafés before catching the ferry across the harbour to downtown Sydney. I maintained my regular routine of creative writing in the Macquarie Street library, followed by visits to the art gallery but found myself lingering longer and longer in the botanical gardens each day as I walked back to Circular Quay. On one particular afternoon in the botanical gardens I noticed a young couple, in their late twenties I suppose, talking, kissing and cuddling in a reasonably respectable way under a tree. The young woman's eyes sparkled as she looked at him adoringly; her hands caressed his face, his hair, his neck, his back, his bottom. Hungry hands wanting to touch all of him and not prepared to settle. She didn't just love him, she adored him. As I watched her adoring eyes I thought of my own marriage to Sheila. I felt reasonably confident that Sheila had loved me in the early days of our relationship but she had never adored me. Her affection had always been a sort of reward exchange for behaviour she wanted and needed from me. I felt more than a little envious as I watched the young couple and resigned myself to the reality that I would never be adored that way.

My next sleepover visit with Sheila in late March was more relaxed than earlier visits and despite being limited to whispered conversations in the bedroom it turned out to be one of the happiest times we had ever spent together. To my great relief Sheila confirmed that Josaphine had given birth to our grandson, without complications. Both mother and child were safe and well. Sheila was bubbling over with excitement, photos and conversation. Our shared time together was both loving and joyful. Despite our difficult circumstances we were two ebullient grandparents celebrating the birth of our grandson, motherhood for our daughter and a new chapter in our lives. Although, of course, I regretted the time I had lost out of Josaphine's life, being unable to share her feelings and provide her with emotional support during the pregnancy and birth, I was also overwhelmed with happiness at many different levels. Sheila assured me that Josaphine was a relaxed, contented new mother who seemed to have a happy relationship with Pete, our new grandson's father and Josaphine's partner.

We knew little about Pete but from what Sheila had observed, he seemed to be a nice enough fellow although he didn't have any money or assets, nor did he have a proper job, describing himself as a professional yachtsman. We understood that he normally lived in the Isle of Wight in England, supporting himself by taking the odd paid position as crew on a yacht when such jobs became available. He also gave sailing lessons and delivered yachts from port to port for a fee. He had told Sheila that he had been visiting Australia as a fringe employee of the England Special Olympics sailing team. He had met Josaphine by chance at our yacht club and a romance had followed. After my disappearance Josaphine had funded a one-month search for my body and he had been heavily involved with that. He had moved into our North Arm Cove home with her during that search period but had returned to the Isle of Wight when Josaphine, at last, ended the search for my body and returned to her apartment in Sydney, resuming her duties as a high school teacher. She then, evidently, visited him in the Isle of Wight during the August school holidays and at that time must have discussed her pregnancy and they reached an understanding about their future together. After that holiday she returned to living and teaching in Sydney. He must have followed her back around Christmas time to be with her in the final phase of her pregnancy and to be present at the birth of their child. Sheila said they intended to return to the Isle of Wight together as a couple to live in a month or two. Josaphine was confident she would easily find work as a teacher and we imagined that in due course he would give up yachting and get a proper job. They were getting on with their lives as any young couple should. It was far from perfect but it all sounded quite promising.

An unexpected benefit for Sheila and I was that they would, for their own reasons, be living in England, only a short distance from the rest of Europe. That geographical proximity would make it so much easier or Sheila and me to have regular contact visits with Josaphine and our new grandson when we started our new life together in Europe. If, after my disappearance, Josaphine had started to build a new life with a different man who needed to stay in Australia, our life together would have been much more complicated.

Another reason for my happiness was a change that seemed to be taking place in Sheila. She seemed, at last, ready to gracefully accept that she was going to grow old, as we all do. I hoped that we both would always take care to be well turned out but perhaps, at last, we could both grow old gracefully together. We took a little time out from our grandparenting conversations to discuss the forthcoming coronial inquest into my disappearance, now expected to take place in April. We decided that once that was behind us we could meet with Josaphine. After some discussion we set a date in May for a two-week family holiday in our North Arm Cove home that would, at last, include Josaphine and our new grandson.

Although Sheila was still anxious that I would be recognised by chance when leaving our Waterloo Street home, our parting, this time, was much more relaxed. We kissed and embraced warmly then I walked out the rear lane back into my other life. I resolved to make significant changes in my routine and subtle changes in my appearance for at least the next 30 days as I was concerned that the upcoming coronial inquest would create more media interest. If my photograph was going to appear on television and in the newspapers again it would be best to lower my profile. I quickly grew a moustache and started wearing large heavy rimmed glasses. I reduced the number of people who both saw me and interacted with me on a daily basis, suspending my ferry trips to Sydney to visit the library, art gallery and botanical gardens. I started wearing a large floppy hat on my daily walks along the promenade and spent much more time alone in the parks that adjoined the northern end of the promenade. I stopped having breakfast in cafés and reduced the time and frequency I spent in the hotel dining room.

I reached a point where I had almost no personal interaction with other people. When the coronial inquest was finally held the media interest, including my photograph on television, seemed to be limited to a single day. That night I searched the faces of my fellow guests in the dining room and listened to their conversations. Nobody made even passing mention of the story and there was not the slightest hint that anyone was interested in me.

That evening I settled in my room with a newspaper to read all the details of the inquest and was astonished to learn that the coroner had made a formal finding that I had drowned. A death certificate would now be issued. I was now officially dead. Sheila and I had considered and discussed this potential outcome but we had always dismissed it as too improbable. Now it was real!

I was dead and there was no going back no matter what we may want.

Within days I felt relaxed enough to go out again and I returned to my former routine, including harbour ferry visits to the city with time in the library, art gallery and botanical gardens each day.

4

Meeting Josaphine

MAY 2001

Sheila collected me from the Pymble Shopping Centre car park and we drove up to North Arm Cove together for our family holiday. She briefed me on a meeting she had with our family solicitor a few days after the inquest and confirmed my understanding of the changed legal situation. Our solicitor had lodged a claim, on her behalf, with AMP for the $3.5 million life insurance claim and had made formal application for probate approval. He expected it to be finalised within three months and wanted her to take formal advice on investments to protect her substantial assets.

Our situation had changed and although we were both surprised we were by no means unhappy with the outcome. After a very brief discussion we agreed that it would be essential to quarantine the insurance payout into a transparent location, and separate it from our other capital for many years, perhaps the remainder of my lifetime. We agreed that the AMP and the police would probably have lingering doubts about my drowning and any attempt to move the life insurance proceeds offshore would just lead a trail to wherever I was living.

We resolved that as soon as the payout was made, Sheila would invest all of it with the AMP Property Trust, that way they would always know where the money was, and it would still be with them. Sheila was very pleased with this plan as it gave her the additional comfort of knowing that if I was ever discovered she would still have the capacity to pay the money back. It was true that Sheila would still have to exercise care when moving our own capital offshore after she sold our assets, but most interest would centre on the insurance payout. Much was resolved between us without any real disagreement but there were still a couple of outstanding issues.

Sheila was unsure when and how to ask for my passport back and was worried how she might explain such a request. She was unsure when she should start selling assets but thought she would probably have to wait for at least three months, perhaps six months after probate. I didn't press her on any of it, she would just have to feel her own way and stay in her own comfort zone. By the time we reached North Arm Cove, some two and a half hours after leaving Sydney, we were settled and could just focus on having a happy family holiday together.

Sheila was the one to tell Josaphine that I was still alive. By the time I met Josaphine she believed I was in a witness protection program. That information coincided with her peripheral knowledge of the pressure I was under from Alek and the Ukrainians prior to my disappearance.

Whatever she knew or believed, it was clear that both she and Pete had been briefed by Sheila as they were both well adjusted to the fact that I was alive before my arrival. Josaphine and I have always been close, so our first meeting was very emotional. We both burst into tears when we first embraced then laughed out loud at the wonderment of life and love. It was a joyful meeting. Although I was concerned that Pete didn't have a proper job and seemed unenthusiastic about work in general he seemed to be a decent and likable fellow. He and I never became close but we quickly developed a warm, functional relationship. That night I met my grandson Chriseb for the first time, starting one of the closest and most loving relationships of my life.

It really was a wonderful family holiday together, despite all the constraints of my personal situation. Sheila never raised her voice in anger and seemed quite comfortable with our company, at times she was almost a loving participant. With music playing on the stereo system I danced for hours with my baby Chriseb in my arms, it was wonderful. We all spent many hours talking together both as a group and in one on one conversation.

In one of my conversations with Josaphine, she asked: 'What really happened Daddy? What is this witness protection program all about?'

'Although I am in a formal program I have been pretty much left to fend for myself,' I replied. 'I really do think it's best if we don't discuss the details, enough to say I have to maintain a low profile and look after myself now. I will probably have to leave the country.'

Josaphine and Pete seemed content to leave it at that – there was very little discussion about the past and a great deal of focus on the future. I outlined my plan to sail from Darwin to Indonesia, probably arriving in August or September.

Although Sheila didn't have a timeline she had a firm sequence in her planning. She told me that she wanted the AMP claim to be paid and reinvested with AMP Property Trust before she started selling other assets to ensure that she didn't become a person of interest to the police or AMP. We hoped the process could be completed not much later than Christmas and then we would fly to Europe as a couple to buy a small hotel in Spain and start our new life together.

We discussed and assured each other how easy and inexpensive it would be for Josaphine, Pete and Chriseb to visit us from their home in the Isle of Wight on a regular basis. Once Josaphine and Pete understood my plan and timeframe they developed their own timeframe to fit with it. We all agreed that we would have a final family holiday at North Arm Cove in early July before Sheila sold it.

Josaphine and Pete decided that they would travel to the Isle of Wight in July immediately after our next holiday at more or less the same time as I would be leaving for Darwin. Although there was significant sadness that after the next holiday together we would never see our North Arm Cove again there didn't seem to be any disagreements between us and we all shared optimism about the future. As is often the case with holidays it all seemed to end too quickly and it was time to leave. Sheila and I had a cheerful drive back to Sydney and kissed warmly when it was time for me to get out in the same Pymble Shopping Centre car park she had collected me from.

5

Becoming Rob

JUNE 2001

I returned to my former routine and my well-established persona of the struggling and unsuccessful author living in the private hotel in Manly trying to write. A couple of days after my return one of the other guests, Rob, unexpectedly engaged me in conversation in the dining room about life in general and literature in particular. Rob told me that he was working as a welder with a local engineering contractor although he was a shipwright by trade and had worked in many varied occupations in his lifetime. He ruefully admitted that he had made some very unwise commercial and romantic decisions in the last few years and now found himself friendless and broke, living in this dreadful hotel at 51 years of age, the same age as me. His particular interest in me was that he knew I was an author. He had a half-written novel, he had been working on for years and he asked me to review it for him. When I protested that I was a most unsuccessful author he laughingly responded: 'Well,

I have been a most unsuccessful husband but I still know a lot more about marriage than an unmarried bloke.' I did read his manuscript and told him, truthfully, that I believed it was very good, but at 20,000 words it was hardly a completed work, it needed volume.

We met regularly after that, often discussing literature and T. E. Lawrence's *Seven Pillars of Wisdom* in particular. We were both avid Lawrence fans and in a couple of our conversations we discussed how he had changed his name to Ross and then Shaw to escape the persona of Lawrence of Arabia. Our relationship grew into a friendship and he accompanied me to the art gallery a couple of times finding that although we were very different people we had lots of common interests and tastes.

I learned that he had lived in Darwin for many years and had sailed to and around many Indonesian islands. Without revealing the exact nature of my situation I asked for his help. 'Rob, can I talk to you confidentially about a very private matter that I could use your help on?'

'Of course Bill, I am not only discreet, I don't have any friends apart from you anyway, whatever I can do to help I will,' he replied without hesitation.

'This is my situation,' I explained. 'I have some legal issues relating to unpaid tax that prevent me from leaving the country with my passport but I need join my family in Europe. I plan to sail a yacht from Darwin to Indonesia in late July without clearing customs and immigration. Once I am in Indonesia I will be able to fly out using my passport because the Indonesian system is not linked to Australia. I would appreciate your help in plotting the safest, quickest route into Indonesia, where I can slip in unnoticed, live on the yacht for a while until I am collected by my wife to fly off to Europe with her. I am a competent harbour sailor and have done some offshore sailing but nothing solo and never in those waters. I could use some help in planning and arranging the trip.'

'You are not a drug dealer wanted by Interpol or anything?' he asked suspiciously.

'Jesus, Rob, of course not. Would a drug dealer be staying in this third-rate hotel, trying unsuccessfully to write?' I responded quickly. 'Rob, I am just another misfit, who can't leave the country because the tax office has a hold on my passport. It wasn't even for a large sum of money. I have never been a big earner, but it's been so long now the penalties will have tripled what I owe, I will never be able to pay it.'

'So how will you live when you get to Europe?' he asked a little less suspiciously.

'Oh my wife's family is wealthy and although I could never ask them to bail me out of a tax problem they are very hospitable and we can stay as long as we like with them. My wife has a small allowance that will be enough for us to live on. We will be all right when we get there. It's just getting out of Australia that is the problem.'

'You aren't planning to do anything illegal when you get there are you?' he replied laughingly, at last convinced that I had no sinister or criminal intentions.

'Of course not,' I replied huffily. 'I have made a mistake in the past but my future intentions are entirely lawful. My wife and I are planning to settle down to a fresh start, her family have even indicated that they may be prepared to buy a small hotel for us to manage, so that we can live nearby but independently from them.'

'Well, nothing wrong with any of that' he replied thoughtfully. 'If Lawrence could change his name for a fresh start I don't see why you shouldn't slip over to Europe for your fresh start. After my run of bad luck I wish I could have a fresh start myself.

Listen, let's talk about this. If you buy a $30,000 yacht in Darwin then sail it to Indonesia, by the time you have paid for the trip then lost some money reselling the yacht the trip will have cost you at least $20,000 and a lot of stress. Why don't I lend you my passport to leave the country and you pay me the $20,000 it would have cost you? You would get your fresh start and the $20,000 would be just what I need to give me my fresh start.'

'What an audacious concept' I thought, and then as I really looked at him it was obvious it wouldn't work.

'We don't even look alike,' I said. 'Gosh you even have blue eyes and mine are brown. No! It would never work.'

'Ha, listen to me my boy,' he said gleefully. 'My passport has expired; it is due for renewal anyway. We can change your eyes to blue with contact lenses. It's true that you will look different to the way I looked 10 years ago but so do I. Back then I was a long-haired hippie, come and look.'

We walked to his room where he produced his old passport. He really had looked like a long-haired hippie in the photo with a beard and drooping moustache. He was right, everyone changes significantly in the 10 years between 40 and 50, but we were the same age, height and build. I too had a full head of hair 10 years ago so why shouldn't he be loosing his hair just the same as I was?

'We can do this,' I thought. I would just need to make myself as much like him as I could, grow a beard, the facial hair would help then have my photo taken at a passport photo shop and send it in with his renewal form, and we could do this.

'I accept, gratefully!' I declared and we shook hands – the deal between us was concluded.

We agreed that because I was now going to grow a beard and moustache plus change the colour of my eyes to blue, it was essential for me to change hotels. I gave a notice at the hotel then stopped shaving and one week later moved to a different private hotel two suburbs away from Manly. Two weeks later, Rob and I met in a rented motel room where we dyed my hair and fiddled with my beard and moustache. We managed to tone down my rather ruddy skin colour with foundation makeup and I had my passport photos taken at a local chemist. We both reviewed the new passport photos alongside the old passport photo and agreed that at a passing glance he may have grown to look like the new passport photo in 10 years but it wouldn't stand serious scrutiny. Rob then provided me with all the identification I would need, including credit cards, Medicare cards, etc. for my meeting with the local justice of the peace.

Despite my anxiety, the meeting with the justice of the peace went very smoothly. He quickly reviewed my supporting identification documents then signed the backs of the photographs as being a true likeness of Rob before completing the referee section of the passport renewal document. Having crossed that hurdle I then went to a travel agent and bought a return air ticket to Frankfurt, Germany, so that I would have a specific departure date for the passport renewal form. I then posted off the form with a photocopy of my airline ticket and a money order for the fee with an expectation that the new passport would be posted to Rob within one month if there were no problems. Rob and I shook hands, wished each other and the application luck then made a date to meet in a café in one month.

Sheila was surprised and delighted by my new changed appearance when she collected me from the Pymble Shopping Centre car park for our last trip to North Arm Cove together. 'You stupid bastard, you should have done this from the very beginning!' she exclaimed. 'It really does make a huge difference and as an added bonus I will be having sex with a different man tonight.'

I recounted to her how my relationship with Rob had developed and although I was going to pay him $20,000 as fair and reasonable compensation for his risk and involvement, it was really an arrangement between friends rather than a commercial transaction.

'He is very different from me, a bit of a rough diamond, but we have become friends,' I went on. I told her about our mutual emotional connection with T. E. Lawrence's need for a name change and a fresh start. She was in good spirits and clearly welcomed this huge improvement in my travel plans.

'You will still need to bring me my Harry Gordon passport,' I told her. 'I can't stay as Rob, it's just a borrowed identity, and the longer I live and travel as Rob the more complicated it will become to change back.' She acknowledged my concern but didn't seem keen to discuss the issue so I let it pass.

Upon my arrival at North Arm Cove I explained to Josaphine and Pete that the witness protection program had decided to provide me with a passport with a new name and that I could fly direct to Europe instead of going via Indonesia in a yacht. We had another wonderful holiday together without any significant anger or tension from Sheila but Josaphine and I felt a little sadness. We visited each room of our home together, around the grounds after dark and out onto the jetty to say goodbye to the home we had built ourselves and had a real bond with. Sheila didn't share our emotional bond with the North Arm Cove home and seemed almost relieved that part of our life was over. All too soon the time together on holiday was over and I again found myself alone in the Pymble Shopping Centre car park.

Rob was relaxed, holding a cup of coffee in his hand. He

smiled broadly at me as I walked into the coffee lounge to meet him. There was a manila envelope on the table in front of him and I instantly understood that it contained the passport. I sat down opposite him and after we exchanged greetings I pulled out a thick yellow envelope and slid it across the table to him. 'Rob, there is $20,000 in there, take it with my fondest wishes. I sincerely hope that the fresh start it gives you takes your life in a direction that brings you health, happiness and security.'

'This is the passport you need for your fresh start,' he replied. 'But I have been thinking about it all and to be quite frank with you I think it is worth $50,000. I don't believe $20,000 is enough.' I opened the manila envelope and studied the passport, it was perfect and it was me.

'Oh Rob, it's worth much more than $50,000,' I said. 'Your gift to me is a priceless opportunity for me to restart my life and I will always be grateful to you. I wish I could afford to pay you the $50,000 but I just don't have that sort of money and have no way of getting it. I think I can spare you another $5,000. It is really going to leave me short but I will manage and Rob, when my wife arrives and we settle down to earn some money I will send you another $5,000. I only wish I could do more Rob, this is a priceless gift, honestly!'

I paused then silently pulled my small carry bag onto my lap. I fumbled inside it before extracting five envelopes, each containing one thousand dollars and passed them to him with my right hand. I had suspected he might try and extract more money from me, as most people do in any deal, so I had brought it with me.

As he took the envelopes from me I placed the passport into my bag with my left hand in a slow deliberate movement leaving no doubt that an exchange was taking place right there in that moment. I could tell from the expression on his face that he was unhappy, but he seemed to understand that he had achieved all that he could; it was now a done deal. We confirmed each other's email details and agreed on a codeword for discussing the passport. We attempted some small talk but the warm fellowship we had once enjoyed was gone, our relationship had been damaged by the financial disagreement and it would never recover. We shook hands, wished each other good fortune but although we exchanged several emails in the following year we have never met since that time.

I gave a great deal of thought to my luggage and personal presentation for the journey out of Australia. I was migrating, not going on vacation, so it was important to take as many of my personal belongings as I could, even if I had to pay some penalty excess baggage costs to the airline. My normal businessman ensemble of dressing in a suit, carrying a suit bag and briefcase was not the look I wanted and would not accommodate the bulky collection of belongings I wanted to take with me. I decided that I was too old to present myself as a backpacker and once again the volume of my belongings would not match that image.

Finally, I decided to think of myself as a man planning a long yachting holiday in a rented yacht once I reached Europe. Even though I had abandoned the idea of sailing from Darwin to Indonesia, I decided that it would explain many of the household items in my luggage if asked by customs.

I bought two large, soft, khaki tubular bags from the army surplus store but was alarmed to find that I couldn't fit everything in. So I bought a third bag against my better judgment, knowing that, lacking three arms, I would always need to use a baggage trolley rather than just carry my bags. This was a substantial mobility disadvantage but, on balance, at that time, it seemed to be the best option. For my personal presentation I decided to wear soft leather boat shoes, smart casual trousers, an open neck shirt with a lightweight windcheater type jacket, all very informal yet quite smart. When I looked at myself critically in the mirror I was well pleased with the result, I looked quite normal.

When, in late July 2001, it was time for my departure, I was far more nervous than I had anticipated. Just getting the blue contact lenses in my eyes turned out to be a huge ordeal. I became hot and flustered and regretted not practising fitting them more often. Thank goodness I had bought six sets as I lost three lenses in that single fitting. To compensate for any unexpected traffic delays I ordered an early taxi pickup. Far too early as it turned out. I arrived at the airport three hours before my scheduled departure instead of the two hours that I had intended.

Although my time at the airport was uneventful I found the whole experience to be a nerve-racking ordeal. Apart from the fact that I had used this airport often in the past and risked being remembered by one of the airport or airline staff, I also understood that on any given day there could, by chance, be several people who knew me personally using the airport – that was just a law of averages and I felt really exposed. As soon as I completed my check in and paid for my excess baggage, I made my way through the customs and immigration desk, then onto the international transit area. There was no problem of any kind, it had all been routine and the new passport had barely been glanced at. I was relieved to find one of the public toilets empty when I entered. I quickly removed my contact lenses in front of the mirror knowing for certain that I couldn't leave them in for the long flight ahead.

6

A fresh start in Europe

JULY 2001

I settled myself into the corner of the airport bar with my head behind a newspaper and sipped slowly on a single glass of champagne for the next two hours. 'So far so good' I said to myself but the anxiety didn't leave me until I was on the aeroplane and it had actually left the runway. The relief was so profound that I gave a small involuntary giggle as the wheels came up.

My good humour about the problem-free departure was worn away by the 10-hour grinding aeroplane trip to Singapore where I took a room in the transit area airport hotel for a shower and a quick lie down. All too soon it was time to face the next gruelling 12-hour leg of the flight to Frankfurt. Most of the flight passed in an uneventful blur but the last two hours seemed to last two lifetimes, it always does. I was so exhausted from the flight that I didn't have the energy or level of anxiety to try and fit my blue contact lenses in on my arrival. I just blundered through customs where my passport was checked in only the most cursory manner without a second glance at my brown eyes. Almost before I understood what had happened I was cleared through into the public arrivals section of the airport. What a relief. I was free and clear in Europe. As soon as Sheila arrived to join me our new life together could start. At that point it became clear that choosing to travel with three bags was foolish. The sheer volume and weight of the bags made it too difficult to even take a simple train trip to the city. I needed to travel by taxi. I had visited and driven in Frankfurt several times in the distant past and although I didn't know the city well I had a loose memory of its layout. With no fuss at all I found a three star hotel in downtown Frankfurt and settled in to recover from the journey.

I spent three wonderful days in Frankfurt just being a tourist. The beer halls and public square marquees were full of locals and tourists enjoying the heat and holiday atmosphere of Frankfurt in mid summer. I bought a mobile telephone and emailed my new number to Josaphine so that I would be contactable. I considered taking the train for the next leg of my journey down to Spain but once again handling my excessive luggage would have made the journey too difficult and anyway, I had to buy a car sooner or later so what better place to buy a car than Frankfurt, the home of Mercedes Benz?

After scouring at least 20 second-hand car yards I bought a second hand Mercedes Benz station wagon. It was a little older than I liked but it was in excellent condition and had the added benefit of being powered by a small, sturdy, economical diesel engine. It cost A\$10,000 to purchase, with an additional and unexpected A\$2,500 to insure and register it. Just a couple of hours after I left Frankfurt on my trip south the air conditioner stopped working and the loss of it certainly diminished some of my touring pleasure through the breathtaking beauty of southern Germany and France.

The regions that I drove through on that journey seem to have a ridiculously short summer but during that brief period it was at times a blisteringly hot 37°C outside and +40°C for me inside the car sitting on the black upholstery. As I crossed over the border from Germany into France in the afternoon of my first day, I selected a freeway exit at random then drove leisurely along the country roads in the district of Baume les Dames with all the windows and sun roof open. In the early evening I stopped at a wonderful French country inn in a picturesque pasture of long, waving, vivid green grass that was mixed with yellow pasture flowers. It seemed almost too beautiful to be real.

I dined that night in a village restaurant that was humming with activity. There didn't appear to be any other tourists as I ate in the company of at least 20 tables of local rural folk who were dining out that night. There was a great deal of good humoured repartee between the tables with lots of laughter and kissing of cheeks. It was a pleasure to be in their contagious good humour. In my dealings with the waitress I found myself having to point at the items on the menu I wanted to eat. The 50-odd words of French I remember from school never seem to be understood by French people, perhaps it is the way I pronounce them. I adore the beautiful French countryside; I love French food and wine. I like the French people and I enjoy the way they live but I suspect they are just a little precious when it comes to understanding the pronunciation of their language by a foreigner.

The next day I continued my country road tour until I arrived at Montpellier on the south coast of France. I stayed the night in a horrible, cheap hotel as I was too tired to look for anything better. I was starting to become unwell and I thought I may be suffering from mild heat exhaustion from spending too many hours in a hot car in mid summer without an air conditioner. The heat may have been part of the problem but I was to learn later that my heath issues were more serious than just heat.

After an early breakfast the next morning I drove down into Spain, my new home. As I was driving the car I became very light-headed and was forced to turn off the freeway to have an urgent rest stop in Gerona, where I actually lost consciousness a couple of times just sitting in the car. I didn't know it at the time but I was having a series of very mild mini strokes and they had diluted some of my cognitive skills. I recovered early enough in the afternoon to continue my journey but I wasn't thinking clearly enough to take the correct freeway exit into Barcelona. I didn't understand my condition then, but learned later that I was in fact hallucinating at the time and shouldn't have been driving at all. I took an exit, any exit and found myself driving along a very busy road in an industrial, commercial district. There didn't appear to be any suitable place to pull over to rest in order to clear my muddled head, it took all my concentration just to drive the car and maintain my position within the busy flow of traffic. At a fork in the road, for no particular reason I turned right following a sign to Sabadell, a town I had never heard of before.

With a huge effort I remained conscious guiding the car along in the busy traffic flow then, without notice, the busy narrow road emptied out onto a slow-flowing boulevard. There was a mix of old and modern elegant buildings on both sides of the boulevard and it was clear that I had arrived in swish, downtown Sabadell. As if in answer to my unuttered prayer I noticed a huge five-star hotel on my side of the road with short-term parking out in front of it. The desk clerk checked me in with flawless English and gave me directions to the entry of the hotel underground car park. It was all effortless and normal, the way fine hotels are all over the world.

Once I was inside my luxury suite I ran myself a cool bath and sat in it for about an hour vomiting and weeping. In due course I emptied the bath, showered off the vomit and cleaned myself up. As I dried myself off and dressed I ordered aspirin, tomato sandwiches and a bottle of champagne from room service. When it arrived I took six aspirin, ate a sandwich and drank half a glass of champagne. Perhaps it was the bath, the air-conditioned room, the aspirin or refreshments but whatever the cause I felt my head clearing and my cognitive skills returning with some energy.

'You need to get a grip of yourself Harry!' I said to myself out loud as I reviewed my situation. 'You are unwell and it is probably more serious than heatstroke. Perhaps you have a virus so you will need medical care but that is not your most urgent problem. Cash flow is your critical problem. You are currently staying in a $400 per night hotel suite, with meals and tips that could easily reach $600 per day. If you continue to stay here most of your money will be gone in a month and then you will be in real trouble. More trouble than you can imagine. Harry, you need to rent a flat and move from this address and move quickly!'

I had about $20,000 left in my cash reserves.

When I felt well enough to come downstairs in the early evening, all the shops and offices of Sabadell reopened for afternoon trading after their siesta so I had time to do business. The hotel desk clerk responded to my request for information regarding real estate letting agents with his personal recommendation. 'Sir, the name for a real estate letting agent in Spanish is *inmobiliaria*. There are very many in

Sabadell, I will give you directions to a reputable one that is within close walking distance of this hotel.' With his excellent directions I arrived at an office just 10 minutes away from the hotel. The real estate letting agent, who spoke no English at all, had been telephoned by the desk clerk to expect me and had a Spanish/English dictionary on her desk in anticipation. Despite the fact that we didn't share any common words we conducted our business with remarkable efficiency. Very soon into the interview, for security and cultural reasons, she advised me against renting one of the really cheap flats on the fringe of town. She showed me instead a rather glamorous newly refurbished one bedroom apartment on the first floor, above a tapas bar of a modern building right in the fashionable centre of town. It was just off the town square. Although it was empty when she showed it to me with the assistance of her translation dictionary she explained that the owner would furnish it for me at no extra cost.

It was perfect and I told her on the spot that I would accept it. We returned to her office where I paid her a total of around A$4,000. It was two months' rent, an additional two months' rent as a bond, and one months' rent as her letting fee, the latter certainly well deserved for a job well done. I returned to the hotel with a spring in my step feeling more than a little pleased with myself. Although I could clearly remember every item that I had packed, I emptied out all three bags in the hotel room that night in a sort of ceremonial stocktake before making a list of all the minor household items I would need to purchase the next day.

I still wasn't well the following morning and needed more aspirin to clear my muddled head but I was out and about a little after nine o'clock. There was a high quality department store in the shopping centre just down the boulevard from the hotel and it was there that I bought all my basic household requirements of bedding, pots, pans, cutlery and crockery. Although I limited my purchases to the absolute minimum, I was alarmed at the expense but it had to be done. I collected the key from the real estate agent then returned to the hotel before packing everything into the Mercedes Benz, including my three bags from the room, before checking out. I was unsurprised and quite philosophical when the hotel bill was even more than I had estimated. 'The service was fantastic but just imagine what it would have cost you if you stayed for a week,' I mused out loud as I walked back to the car.

The only significant downside of my new fashionable inner city address was that it had no private parking arrangements but after circling the block several times I managed to find a vacant parking space about half a kilometre away from the apartment. It took several hours, six trips to the car and one to the local supermarket before I could actually declare myself 'moved in'. Despite the fact that I was most unwell I forced myself to continue as I was not prepared to stop until everything was put away – clothing in the wardrobe, pots etc. in the cupboards and food in the fridge. When I was at last satisfied that all the tasks were completed, I collapsed with exhaustion and didn't wake until dawn the following morning. I was still unwell so over coffee and toast with my Spanish/English dictionary I prepared a note.

'My name is Rob. I am an Australian citizen living in Sabadell. I am not a tourist. I am sick and need medical assistance. I have money and can afford to pay. My symptoms include a high temperature, fever and nausea. I can't concentrate and one of my arms seems to tingle then go numb every now and then. Perhaps I have the flu. Please prescribe antibiotics.'

After breakfast with my note in hand I set out to find help.

The first medical centre I found could not help me for reasons that are still unclear but they gave me directions to another centre within walking distance. The second medical centre, with a large blue cross in its window, turned out to be workplace injury specialist and they couldn't help either but gave me directions to the Sabadell Public Hospital. After a lot of fuss and bother in the reception area I was at last ushered in to see the doctor.

He was a short man of slight build in his mid-forties with shining bright brown eyes. The open neck shirt he wore under his white dust coat seemed slightly out of keeping with his serious attitude. He stood at full attention as he read my note several times and looked me up and down. 'Ah yes, very good, very good,' he uttered each time he read it. Then with limited English he explained that he was from Palestine and with God's help he had qualified as a doctor after much study and hardship thus he was well qualified to assist me. He took a very strange looking torch out of his desk, more suited to an automotive toolkit, and looked in each of my ears then my throat for good measure. 'Ah yes, very good' he murmured each time before placing a thermometer in my armpit.

About this time we were joined in the room by a stern looking lady who must have been his supervisor. Although I didn't understand a word they spoke to each other it became clear to me that she was telling him that he was not supposed to treat an Australian tourist in a public hospital. She pointed at me then to the door before storming out. He was clearly shaken and more than a little flustered by the encounter. He looked at me then the doorway where she had just left. 'Oh dear, what to do? What to do?' I could almost hear him thinking. It is to his great credit that he resolved the ethical conflict very quickly all by himself. He squared his shoulders and stiffened his back as he stood to his tallest attention before resuming the examination. He had clearly decided that his primary duty was to his patient rather than his supervisor.

He believed I had two unrelated medical conditions. The first was a simple virus of some kind that was easy to treat. He found some hospital stationery and on a very old pink typewriter he prepared a prescription for the chemist before stamping it several times with a variety of rubber stamps. He was far more concerned, he said, by the symptoms that indicated I had probably suffered a series of minor strokes that needed the attention of a cardiovascular specialist but that probably could and should wait until the virus cleared up. In the short term he prescribed 100 milligrams of aspirin to be taken daily and another medication that I had never heard of. 'In a few days when the virus is improved you must find yourself a personal doctor in Sabadell, it cannot be me, it must be private practice. Your doctor will refer you to a specialist.' I think that is what he said! I pulled out my wallet and offered payment but he waved it away as if money would sully him. He had just been tested in an ethical conflict of interest and had come out a bigger and better man for it. He looked as if he believed this was his finest hour. Perhaps it was.

I collected my medication from a high street chemist on my way back to the apartment and once home I put myself to bed for three days of total rest. On the fourth morning, although not fully recovered, for the purpose of engaging with the outside world I declared myself cured. After eating a hearty breakfast of bacon and eggs with steaming hot coffee I took myself downstairs to explore Sabadell. Although the activity was, by later standards, a little subdued with many of the businesses closed for the summer vacation, I found that Sabadell was a busy, sophisticated, modern city with lots of colour and movement. Everything I saw pleased me. I liked the place and I liked the people, I still do. I was later to learn that although Sabadell is a major industrial and commercial centre, not a backwater, because it has no cathedral or buildings of historic significance, tourists are not drawn to visit it. This lack of tourist activity seemed to suit the citizens of Sabadell and it certainly suited me as there was almost no chance that I would ever encounter another Australian let alone one who knew me.

It was a perfect location for me to live anonymously. I reflected on my good fortune at finding this place. An accidental choice at a literal fork in the road had delivered me to this place, how fortunate indeed. Upon my return to the apartment I found that the tapas restaurant and bar directly below my apartment was open and humming with activity. On impulse I decided to go in for a beer or two to celebrate my new home and the restoration of my good health. I walked into the bar, perched myself on a bar stool. 'I'll have a beer thanks mate,' I said pointing at the beer taps then I remembered a Spanish phrase from a *Terminator* movie so I added '*Hasta la vista* baby!'

The barman smiled as he wordlessly pulled me a beer then as he placed it in front of me he said, 'Open the window.' I was to learn later that it was the only English phrase he could remember from his childhood language classes at school. Some hours and several beers later, I had acquired a functional vocabulary of about 20 Spanish words from my Spanish only conversation with the barman and several of the patrons. It became a daily routine for me to call in at the same bar at about the same time each evening for a beer. Within two months I had developed friendships and a vocabulary of about 500 words, both from within that bar.

Those months were a really joyful time for me, my health had returned and I no longer had the stress of being in hiding.

I explored every street of Sabadell on foot and spent many hours in the wonderful park. I attended every fete and festive event that was held in the town square each week. More than 100 faces became familiar to me and I knew I was familiar to them; I was becoming connected, making a home. One evening I was sitting in a café on the edge of the town square just before a fiesta within a group of people who were all familiar to me from regular contact. We noticed a woman, a stranger, walking through the square. She was wearing red shoes, blue jeans, a yellow blouse, a green jacket and carrying a brown bag. One of the ladies in our group leaned across and said to me: 'Oh dear, the English women are so special aren't they?' It was of course wickedly funny and the entire group giggled but more importantly for me, at that moment, I knew I had been included in the group. I was no longer a stranger. I had told them I was looking at potential property investments.

My imperfect and incomplete language skills were never an impediment to developing relationships but there were at times significant and often amusing misunderstandings. One evening in conversation with a group I was explaining that I had been clumsy in some matter I used the phrase '*Todos dedos y pilger*' that loosely translates to a common English phrase 'I am all fingers and thumbs'. The group immediately went silent and several of the ladies raised their eyebrows with bemusement. One of the women sighed then murmured '*Ah si! Todos dedos y pulger*' more wistfully than seemed decent and I grasped the confused context with embarrassment before adding hastily 'No, no, it is my poor translation, sorry, not sexual!' They all collapsed in gales of laughter as they often did during my tortured Spanish sentences.

I drove the 25-minute trip into Barcelona almost every week. I spent time in the cathedral and over time I explored every street and laneway of the old city, soaking up the history. I visited and marvelled at all of Gaudi's buildings, dizzy with delight at the undulating facades and moved to wonderment at the beauty of his parabolic arches, profoundly aware of and humbled by his genius. During the heat of the summer I swam in the Mediterranean Sea, either in Barcelona or at one of the many towns on the coastal road North of Barcelona.

On one of my touring trips up the northern coastal road I discovered the seaside town of Tossa de Mar and fell in love with it. Sabadell was a lovely city but this was something completely different and far better suited to the new life that Sheila and I would build together. I resolved that if Sheila agreed, we should buy one of the small hotels that was for sale in Tossa de Mar. Perhaps it could be our commercial future. That arrangement would allow us four months of each year as a couple for completely personal family time of relaxation, reflection as well as time to be with Josaphine and our grandson. If Sheila needed to make an annual pilgrimage to Australia and New Zealand to visit her family she could also fit that in. Although I would leave Sabadell with more than a little sadness, it was a comfort to know that we would still be still close enough to maintain contact and occasional visits with some of my new Spanish friends so the move would not be another complete upheaval and abandonment of emotional contacts. The future seemed very clear. I couldn't wait to show Sheila and Josaphine. I felt sure that they would fall in love with it as I had.

Apart for my touring and exploring I had a specific task in Barcelona twice each week. Each week I would visit one of the many internet cafés in Barcelona to receive and respond to emails from Josaphine. On another day of the week at prearranged times I would telephone her on her mobile telephone from a public telephone booth. I would have liked to have a similar arrangement with Sheila but she had rejected the idea as being bad risk management.

'If something important comes up or there is an emergency I will contact Josaphine and she can contact you, nobody is watching her, all the fucking eyes are on me,' she had said in one of the conversations before I left.

'I don't really want to get Josaphine too involved in the details of our arrangements. She has her own life now with Pete,' I had replied.

'Don't you worry about that, I won't be discussing any of my business with her but she can get a message to you if there is an emergency,' she replied emphatically.

Although most of the emails and telephone calls between Josaphine and I were simply to satisfy each other that we were safe and well, we also made arrangements for her to travel from the Isle of Wight to have a one-month holiday with me in Sabadell. We discussed the normal domestic implications to her relationship of spending a week away from Pete and the risk-management issues associated with visiting me. Josaphine was far more casual about the whole thing than I was. She probably had a different take on the legal implications than I did because she still believed I was in a witness protection program of some kind. In any event, we agreed on the arrangements.

On one of those communication trips to Barcelona my Mercedes Benz was stolen. I had parked it in a normal one-hour parking space in a busy street of downtown Barcelona. It was not secluded at all, in fact it was a high visibility location. I returned to the parking space from the internet café about a half hour later than the allowed hour and although I feared that it may have been stolen I hoped that it may have been towed away by the parking police.

I attempted to report the loss at the nearest police station but the unfortunate combination of an impatient police desk officer and my poor Spanish language skills prevented communication between us and I was referred to the central police station where multilingual police officers specialised in dealing with tourist-related crime. An attractive young female officer to took my details and went to check if the car had been towed away due to a parking issue. When she returned she spoke to me in a very sympathetic and respectful manner as if she were speaking to an elderly uncle. 'I am so sorry Sir!' she said with just the hint of a lisp. 'The parking police did not take your beautiful Mercedes Benz, I am afraid it has been stolen, you must be so very sad at this terrible news, I really am most sorry for you!'

I was indeed sad. My German $2,000 insurance did not cover the loss by theft in another country. After the loss sank in, the young officer and I formally filled out the stolen car form together. I was surprised to find that although the form detailed my personal information and the make, model and colour of the car, it did not record the engine or chassis numbers and since I had access to those details in my carry bag I asked: 'Surely you will need these details? Otherwise all the thief needs to do is re-register the car and nobody will ever know it was my car.'

'This is a problem with our system I know sir,' she replied sadly, touching my arm with empathy. 'This is probably why we hardly ever recover foreign cars stolen from tourists. It is all very sad.' What could I say to that? I caught the train home to Sabadell feeling very sad and sorry for myself. As expected, the car was never recovered and I had to quickly adjust to using public transport. I was shocked to discover how much easier and cheaper it was than using a car. The central Sabadell underground train station was just a five-minute walk from my apartment, much closer and less stressful than my normal parking arrangements. In peak times the train to Barcelona ran every half hour and in off peak times every hour. The train took me right to La Rambla in the centre of downtown Barcelona with no parking issues or rush to return to the car as there had been when I used the Mercedes Benz. I shook my head in wonder at my earlier foolishness, it really was much easier.

As we had arranged, Josaphine and Chriseb arrived in late October to spend a one-month holiday with me in Sabadell. It was a wonderful time for all of us and we rejoiced in each other's company and they were quickly accepted into the groups of acquaintances and friends that I had in Sabadell. The women in particular made a great fuss over Chriseb and I was happy to confirm their opinion that he was indeed beautiful. With all the enthusiasm of a dedicated tourist guide, I showed off the sights and delights of both Sabadell and Barcelona to Josaphine, every day was filled with excitement with so much to see and do.

We rented a car and drove up the coast so that I could show off Tossa de Mar to Josaphine and share my plan for her mother and I to buy a small hotel there. As I expected Josaphine was enchanted by it. 'Oh Daddy this is a magic place,' she exclaimed. 'Once you and mum settle in we will come and spend every summer vacation with you. What a wonderful place for Chriseb to spend the long hot summers of his childhood.' On the drive back to Sabadell she advised me that Pete was keen for them to relocate their base from the Isle of Wight to Alacudia in Majorca where he felt there would be more opportunities for him to obtain constant work as a sailing instructor, as his work in the Isle of Wight was limited to the very short English summer season.

Although Josaphine loved the idea of living in Spain she had some well-founded misgivings about the financial implications of the move. She had always been aware that Pete's income would be spasmodic and unreliable therefore her income as a teacher would be vital to the long-term stability of their household budget. She had intended to return to work as soon as Chriseb turned one and while it was easy for her to secure teaching work in the Isle of Wight, where there was a teacher shortage, she wasn't qualified to teach in Spain and didn't even speak the language.

She understood that even after she learned Spanish, her employment prospects on Majorca were uncertain at best. 'It would be wonderful to live in Spain, I love the country, the people, the climate, the food and you would only be a half day ride away in the ferry but I really don't know if the money would work,' she mused.

'I suppose we can give it a try and if it doesn't work out we can always move back to the Isle of Wight can't we?' she concluded. All too soon it was time for the holiday to end and to think about planning our next holiday together. We knew that Sheila had firm plans to fly to the Isle of Wight in late December to celebrate Christmas with Josaphine, Chriseb and Pete. From her cryptic clues we understood that she would probably fly over to visit me after that. We had no idea where she was up to with probate and/or the sale of assets, nor her timeframe for moving from Australia to Spain to settle in our new life together.

After Josaphine left, I calculated my cashflow requirements against my reserves. I had become quite concerned that I was running out of money and if for some reason Sheila was delayed I could be in real trouble. I became more frugal in my day-to-day activities and started to make some tentative enquiries about employment opportunities. I learned that there was a substantial surplus of unskilled migrant labour in Spain from North Africa, some with valid visas and some without. These people flowed into the menial unskilled labour jobs so it was pointless me trying to compete for that sort of work. Until I improved my limited language skills and resolved how to qualify for a work visa, I would be unable to secure the type of semi-skilled clerical or trade position that I would be most suited to.

I did discover, however, that if I improved my written Spanish language skills there was some hope of me securing employment as a real estate salesman in one of the coastal resort towns selling holiday homes, mostly to English people. Although I had no reason to suppose that Sheila wouldn't arrive in time to replenish my cash reserves, I settled down to study Spanish as winter closed in.

The weather became much colder in December than I had anticipated and the locals confirmed that it was the coldest winter they had experienced in Catalonia in many years. The landscape became beautifully dusted with several light snowfalls and the rail journey into Barcelona was interrupted several times due to ice on the lines, adding an element of excitement without any great inconvenience. Delightful temporary market stalls were set up in La Rambla of Sabadell, selling all of the normal Christmas festive decorations. There were public and private bright-coloured Christmas lights everywhere and familiar Christmas tunes were playing on the public address systems of stores and sidewalks. It really felt like Christmas and as this has always been a special time of year for me I enjoyed all the sights and delights of it, regretting only that I couldn't share it with Sheila, Josaphine and our grandson. 'Next year we will have a real Christmas together as a family,' I told myself as I ate my Christmas dinner alone in the apartment.

I continued my weekly talk and email with Josaphine and she confirmed that she and Pete were definitely relocating to Alacudia in the first week of the new year. We spoke on

Christmas Day, exchanging messages of love and festive greetings before she passed the telephone to Sheila so that we could do the same. The conversation with Sheila was brief and rather strained, she explained that she was talking outside in the cold without warm clothes and needed to hurry back indoors. Josaphine explained that Sheila was planning to accompany them on their move to Alacudia and notwithstanding the risk-management issues, I was invited to come and stay with them in their new home, to reconnect with Sheila and for us all to spend time together as a family.

I caught the ferry on the appointed day but due to a minor geographical misunderstanding I travelled to Palma, at the wrong end of Majorca, instead of Alacudia. After a long taxi ride and several mobile telephone conversations, I arrived at their new home at about 10 o'clock that night. I received a loving welcome from Josaphine as always, but the reception from both Pete and Sheila was barely more than civil. There were obvious tensions between all the parties in the household. Pete and Josaphine were caught up in some sort of domestic dispute and were barely on speaking terms with one another and Sheila was exasperated with both of them. It was extremely awkward for all concerned until at last it was mercifully time for bed.

When Sheila and I were at last in bed together she whispered endlessly about every minor indignity she imagined that she had suffered as their house guest. 'Who the hell do they think that they are?' she asked before offering an analysis of all Pete's flaws as a man, then Josaphine's flaws as a woman, daughter and mother before giving a final dissertation on their flaws as a couple. In due course we drifted off to sleep without kissing let alone making love. The next two days in Alacudia continued in the same atmosphere of barely restrained hostility between the parties until it was time for Sheila and me to catch the ferry to Barcelona followed by the suburban train to my apartment in Sabadell.

I was very aware that my already fragile relationship with Sheila had been strained by the separation so I was careful not to take offence at her sometimes difficult behaviour and made every effort to be thoughtful and loving in all of my words and actions. She very quickly made it clear to me that her move to Spain was still some time off as she had not yet started selling any of the assets. She indicated that our family solicitor was still dealing with AMP on the insurance and some formal probate issues. Perhaps because I didn't press her on the details of this, within two days of our arrival in Sabadell our relationship seemed to return to some sort of normality. We made love every night. Our conversations flowed easily both in the evenings and during the days when we went on outings for me to show off the sights and delights of Sabadell and Barcelona. With each passing day Sheila seemed to relax a little more as we both enjoyed the place, the food, the people and the carefree holiday atmosphere of our time together.

I hired a car and we drove up the coast to Tossa de Mar where I explained my proposal for us to purchase one of the small hotels there for our new life together. Although she was not overly enthusiastic, Sheila agreed that it was generally a suitable plan and place. Her primary and valid concern was to ensure there would be enough local people who spoke English for her to have some social interaction, as she didn't believe she would ever learn either Spanish or Catalonian and didn't want to be isolated by language. It didn't take us long to establish that unlike Sabadell, Tossa de Mar was a real tourist town and lots of the locals spoke several languages. She seemed satisfied but restrained.

I had been expecting Sheila to bring me at least A$20,000 to replenish my cash reserves, but was hopeful that she may bring me as much as $50,000 if she wasn't going to join me for a few months. I was both shocked and hurt when she handed me an envelope containing A$4,000 on the day of her departure. I felt betrayed and more than a little frightened about my immediate future.

'Don't worry, I will be back in a few months with some more money,' she said. 'In the meantime you will just have to live within a tighter budget and learn to make do,' she instructed me without the slightest hint of embarrassment. We kissed goodbye at the airport and exchanged all the normal endearments but my heart really wasn't in it as I reflected on how fragile my position had become.

After Sheila left I applied and was appointed for the real estate selling position on the coast with a start in late January. This position had the potential to generate a significant commission income for me but it was highly seasonal. Most of my potential customers were English visitors who made their initial contact with our office during the July to September summer vacation season. Although I knew it would be a very lean period for me over the next few months, the commission from just one or two sales would make all the difference to my financial situation if Sheila let me down again. I would be up and running to support myself completely once the peak season arrived.

I settled down to work on all the 'cold sale' files my new boss made available to me. I had one sale completed and was starting to make some real progress with another three prospects by February when I needed to change my plan to suit a change in Josaphine's situation. Josaphine came to visit me and told me that she and Pete seemed to have irreconcilable differences in their relationship and she believed it was ending. She intended to return to Pete for one last attempt to work things out between them, but really didn't hold any serious hope that she would succeed.

'If it doesn't work out can Chriseb and I come and live with you?' she asked. Although at that particular time and place it would be extremely inconvenient for me financially I replied: 'Of course my darling daughter. Wherever I am in the world, my home is always your home, that's the way family works, never, ever doubt it.'

Although we both adored Spain it was clear to me that if her relationship with Pete failed, as now seemed probable, we would run out of money if we remained in Spain. We decided to relocate to the UK where both of us could easily and quickly secure employment. We decided that I should go to England ahead of her to find a job and a place to live so that she and my grandson could join me if she was unable to patch things up with Pete.

Because there was no prospect of me obtaining a work visa to work in England I asked Pete, by telephone, if I could use his name and tax file number for the remainder of the financial year. Although it is doubtful that he would have consented had he known that Josaphine was planning to leave him, after confirming that it was a short-term loan and that I would pay the proper rate of tax, he gave his consent and provided me with the tax file number. I was probably more concerned with the arrangement than he was and one of my father's often used phrases came to mind: 'Oh what a tangled web we weave when first we practise to deceive.'

7

Living in Wigan

MARCH 2002

Josaphine and I did an internet search together and after
finding that a labour hire company in Wigan, a town, midway
between Liverpool and Manchester in the north of England,
was advertising a number of easy entry jobs we decided that
it would be as good as any other place to set up our base. In
March I flew into Luton airport and caught a train to Wigan
and found my way to the bed and breakfast private hotel that
I had booked for myself over the internet. Within 24 hours of
my arrival I found and moved myself from the private hotel
into a small and rather primitive single room flatette. There
was a shower compartment, basin and hotplate cook top in the
room along with a bed, lounge chair and coffee table. It was less
than basic but at 60 pounds a week the price was right. I quickly
made contact with the labour hire company that had advertised
on the internet and within two days I was given a temporary
one-week placement in a vegetable processing factory. It was

an awful, dirty job and poorly paid but at long last I had a real income of my own.

The following week the labour hire company manager gave me a semi-permanent placement as an 'order filler warehouseman' at a potato crisp warehouse. Although it was still a very physically demanding job it was a vast improvement on the vegetable factory. The potato crisp warehouse was about a 20-minute drive out of Wigan and after catching a taxi to work on the first day I managed to hitch a ride with one of the other workers who lived in Wigan but because his shift didn't always coincide with mine it was necessary for me to buy a car. Using almost half my remaining cash reserve I bought and old Volvo for a thousand pounds.

A month after my arrival I arranged a couple of days off around a weekend to give myself a four-day break. I flew to Barcelona then caught a train back to my apartment in Sabadell. I had a 12-month lease so I had to continue to pay the rent.

Josaphine met me there and after farewelling our many acquaintances we emptied out the last of my personal possessions from the apartment, paid the last rent of the tenancy agreement and said our last goodbye to Sabadell with real regret and sadness. 'We will come back to Spain to live won't we Daddy?' asked Josaphine plaintively over a long boozy, seafood lunch in Barcelona. 'I sure hope so,' I replied positively but with vague misgivings that our Spanish adventure may be finished. We kissed and said our sad farewells before Josaphine caught the ferry back to Majorca and I flew on to Manchester.

I quickly settled back into my working life in Wigan and was comforted to see my cash reserves creeping up by more than a hundred pounds a week due to my austere lifestyle. As anticipated, Josaphine informed me in one of our weekly telephone conversations that her differences with Pete were irreconcilable and in mid-April she and Chriseb came to live with me in Wigan.

The one-room flatette was totally unsuitable for the three of us to live in together but we bought a roll-out camper bed and somehow we managed to live there for several weeks until we rented an unfurnished three-bedroom home in a run-down part of Wigan. The bond, rent and purchase of second-hand furniture used all of our cash reserves so we moved in with just a couple of hundred pounds available for emergencies.

Josaphine found an employment agency that specialised in placing teachers in work and was quickly offered temporary work at a high school in Wigan. We needed to completely reorganise our lives to make it work. I applied and was accepted for a quality control inspector's job at the vegetable processing factory where I had worked in my first week because it was within walking distance of our new home. I resigned my position at the potato crisp warehouse and was able to start my new job within a week. Because I was able to walk to work, Josaphine used our little Volvo car to go to and from the Wigan High School where she started teaching. We found a suitable daycare nursery for Chriseb close to home. Josaphine dropped him off on her way to work each day and because my work shift was from 6.00am until 2.30pm each day I was able to collect him each afternoon at around 3.00pm and push him home in a stroller.

Although it seemed hectic at first, within a couple of weeks we settled into a comfortable domestic routine and our cash reserves quickly improved, with two incomes coming into the household. My job required me to work six days a week with Sundays off. Josaphine used Saturday as her day of rest and domestic tasks leaving us every Sunday free for a touring adventure. Although we were careful with our spending,

111

we travelled far and wide throughout the United Kingdom, including the delights of the Lakes District and lower Scotland as well as the wonderful beaches, coastal villages and castles of Wales.

Every Sunday afternoon, wherever we were, Josaphine telephoned Sheila in Australia from a callbox. She indicated that Sheila sounded a bit disconnected asking few questions herself and offering no news of any kind. In one of the conversations, however, Sheila did indicate that she was flying over to visit in late June and gave details of her flight so that she could be collected from Heathrow airport.

The three months that Josaphine, Chriseb and I spent together that spring as a family as we waited for Sheila to arrive was a wonderful carefree time for all of us. Although aspects of my job were unpleasant I adjusted, settled in and made the best of it taking a real interest in my work and the people I worked with.

The company sent me on a formal food-hygiene training course and after giving me a small pay rise my supervisor suggested I should aspire to promotion within the company. It was all most satisfactory. Josaphine too had a happy work and social experience at the high school in Wigan. We found ourselves quickly accepted into the community with people I knew from work and parents of Josaphine's high school students often stopping to chat with us in the street or the supermarket aisle.

We often popped into the local pub for a beer and a lemonade for Chriseb in the evenings where we always encountered people who knew us and wanted to chat making us feel included in the community. It was also a real bonding time for Chriseb and me, especially in the afternoons on the walk home from the daycare nursery. We always stopped at the local shop to select an ice cream each with a great deal of ceremony. I was puzzled why the female shop assistant always called me 'Milo' as she was serving me then after a couple of weeks I realised she was actually saying 'My love'. As we were eating our ice cream on the way home Chriseb and I often stopped at a bridge over the canal to inspect any new barges that had arrived. We became and remain very close to one another.

In anticipation of Sheila's visit I requested a one-week holiday from work to coincide with her scheduled time with us. Josaphine's school would be on holiday at that time so she was also free to spend time with her mother. We didn't know what news Sheila would bring but we were very much looking forward to her visit and the prospect of being a complete family again. We speculated endlessly with one another on when Sheila would complete the sale of assets so that we could all return to start life together as a family in Spain. We were both very excited about the visit and our future in general. Sheila had indicated to Josaphine in one of their telephone conversations that during her visit she hoped to spend some time with us touring northern England and wanted to make a visit to London to revisit the suburb where she had lived as a child.

On Sheila's arrival day we travelled down to London to meet and greet her. As basic risk management I waited outside as Josaphine went into the airport terminal to collect her. In due course they came out and we were all in the car together. Sheila seemed stiff and stand-offish with all of us but as it is a 24-hour aeroplane journey from Sydney to London we expected her to be exhausted and didn't take any offence at her behaviour. We chatted away happily about all that had happened to us, our jobs, the people we had met and our touring adventures as she sat almost silent during the long drive back to Wigan.

When we arrived home at last Sheila put her bags away in the master bedroom then asked me to join her in the backyard for a private husband and wife chat while she smoked a couple of cigarettes. She sat down on the chair next to me, lit a cigarette and without pausing began to talk.

'I have come here to end our marriage Harry. I wanted to tell you face to face that I have found someone else to share my life with. After this holiday is over I will return to Australia to get on with my life with him. I hope you have a happy life Harry, I wish you luck. When this holiday is over we will never need to see each other ever again. You need to go inside to tell Josaphine now, she will understand, she is always ending her relationships so it is nothing new to her but it will sound better coming from you.'

Her manner and tone of voice were so emotionless and matter of fact that it took a few seconds for her words to register and the reality of the situation to sink in. My heart started thumping in my chest and I felt like vomiting. 'Please don't do this Sheila,' I asked. 'Whatever the issues are we can work them out, please don't do this to me, to us and to our marriage.' I almost pleaded with her as I struggled for breath.

'Harry. It's over! You are the one who fucked up our marriage with all the shit you brought to it. I am not going to spend the rest of my life with you. I have found someone else to spend my life with, a normal person. I just don't need any more of your shit!'

I composed myself then went inside to tell Josaphine the news as gently as I could. 'It's important that you don't judge your mother too harshly over this. She didn't ask to take this difficult journey with me and it is just too hard for her. She never had that level of commitment to me. She didn't marry me because I was handsome, entertaining or the love of her life. An important part of the deal was that she would have a soft life with a good provider. This journey is too tough for her, she never signed on for better or worse with me so she is opting out of the worse. That's fair and it's her call to make.'

'The bitch! How dare she abandon you after all you have done for her and her awful family over all those years?' Josaphine responded wildly.

'Now you listen to me and get a grip on yourself,' I told her forcefully. 'Your mother has given me the flick and she has moved into a new reality with a new man. The family you used to belong to doesn't exist anymore. She has already moved on emotionally from me, nothing can change that now. Your mother is tougher, harder and smarter than the two of us put together. Your challenge is not to go down with the sinking ship but to leap into the lifeboat of her new reality. You need to get close to her in her new life and her new man to protect your own emotional and financial interests.

'As soon as you can I need you to return to Australia to rebuild your relationship with her. Don't you dare walk away from your inheritance on some judgment trip. I will always love you unconditionally and you will always be safe with me but your mother is a very different person to me and she has moved on. Get a grip kiddo and get into her reality or your inheritance is gone. She will wipe you if you aren't careful, she is harder than you will ever understand, dqn't doubt it!'

Josaphine did get a grip. She moved Chriseb into her bed allowing me to take over his room and we all carried on as if the new arrangement was normal. We went out touring as a family every day occasionally stopping overnight in a motel but mostly we returned home each evening. We took in the Lake District, Oxford and Sheila's childhood haunts in London. It was heartbreaking for Josaphine and me knowing that this was the last time we would ever be together as a family but

Sheila seemed to enjoy the sights and delights with robust good humour and no apparent emotional anxiety. She just didn't seem to feel the same way as us, she probably never had and perhaps our expectations had always been unrealistic and unreasonable. On the day before Sheila was due to leave I explained to her that Josaphine's plans had changed.

'Now that our marriage is over and our life together as a family in Spain is no longer an option I will need to make a fresh start for myself. Josaphine needs to return to Australia to be with you as soon as we can make the arrangements,' I explained.

'Why can't she stay with you?' she asked. 'She can't live with me! I have my own life to live,' she argued.

'Now you listen to me,' I said angrily. 'Neither I nor Josaphine are asking you to become your grandson's babysitter. You have ended our marriage, not me Sheila, this isn't my doing. You have ended the marriage! I accept the marriage is over and I am willing and able to take care of my own needs without your help until you dispose of the assets and give me my half. That may be some time off. I am going to give you some elbow room on that. I am not going to rush you but by God Sheila, in the meantime I expect Josaphine and Chriseb to return to the safety and security of their own family home.'

'It's not their home, it's my home!' Sheila almost spat the words out. 'She is nearly 30 years old, she has her own life, she needs to grow up and get on with it.'

'These are not some strangers,' I argued back. 'This is your own daughter and grandson. Jesus Sheila, I don't suppose the relationship you have with your only child and only grandchild is any of my business anymore but I will tell you this and don't you dare misunderstand me. As long as you are living in our homes using money from our bank account, you will accept responsibility for their welfare, do you understand that Sheila!

It's not negotiable!' She went off to her bedroom to pack in silent rage.

The following morning, knowing that it would be the last time we would ever be together, I drove her to London by myself. In the car, as we travelled, I apologised for the cross words we had exchanged the day before and I made a little speech thanking her for the 25 years of love and loyalty she had given me. I told her that although I was very sorry that our marriage had ended I wished her a happy future with her new man. Sheila said in reply that all of her marriage to me had been exciting and much of it had been happy.

'You will build another business and make money again. You will marry again Harry, that's the sort of man you are. In a couple of years from now you and your new wife will be out entertaining clients in a restaurant and you will be telling the same stories. You will pay the bill and without looking and leave a big tip then you will blush when one of your client's wives kisses you on the mouth. You won't change! It's been a great ride Harry, lots of excitement, but I want to get off now and have a normal life with a normal man. I don't need to wish you luck, you have always been lucky.'

Our parting was almost affectionate but it was a real parting. Our life together had ended.

When I returned home Josaphine and I spent the evening drinking too much wine and talking endlessly about what it all meant without reaching any meaningful conclusion. I thought of all the things I should have asked Sheila and hadn't. She had indicated that AMP would not be paying out any life insurance claim and she had not given me any solid information about our commercial interests. I realised that I had been too shell-shocked by the news that out marriage had ended to really think about anything else, for some reason none of it seemed important anymore. As Josaphine and I talked the reality dawned that I would need to leave England too. I couldn't continue to use Pete's tax file number and I couldn't acquire a visa to work in England as Rob. Our life in Wigan was defiantly over. So the next morning we began the process of winding it up.

Josaphine was still on a long summer school vacation so giving notice was just a formality for her but I needed to give proper notice. To make the departure less stressful, we decided that I should stay on for a week or so after Josaphine left so that I could run them to the airport on their scheduled departure then return to dispose of the furniture and shut down the tenancy in an orderly manner.

We bought their tickets to Australia and I bought a ticket to South Africa where I knew I would be allowed to work and live with my Australian citizenship of Rob. Josaphine pre-sold all of our furniture to a second-hand dealer who would collect it a couple of days after she left, leaving me just a little stretcher bed so that I would have somewhere to sleep. It was a very sad time for us and all too soon it was time for them to leave. Just 30 minutes into our drive, when we had barely left home on the drive down to Heathrow airport in London, at the most inconvenient time, our little Volvo car broke down for the first and final time. With our eyes on the time and our hearts in our mouths, with agonising delays, we arranged for a tow truck to take us to the nearest town where we left the car with a mechanic to be repaired and hired a car to complete our journey to London.

Instead of a leisurely drive to London with time to talk and have our fond farewells over a leisurely lunch it turned into an anxiety ridden journey with all the focus of our conversation on meeting the airline check in deadline. As soon as we reached the airport Josaphine dashed in without a measured farewell.

Although we had agreed to maintain contact by email each month I had no idea when I would ever see them again. I felt empty and alone driving back to Wigan. I felt I had lost more than my marriage, I had also lost my family, my name and even my future, it was all gone.

The following day I returned the hire car and collected the Volvo. During the next few days I spent many hours after work on the internet researching jobs in South Africa. The process was going to be a lot harder than I had thought. It was clear that although I could obtain a work visa it would take time for me to secure employment because the unemployment rate was so high and I didn't even speak the local language. It suddenly all seemed too risky because I really didn't have enough cash reserves to support myself for too long without an income.

Despite the fact that I couldn't get a refund on my airline ticket, I decided to change my destination from South Africa to New Zealand. Although I didn't need a work visa in New Zealand and was far more confident about securing employment there the big disadvantage was that there was much more risk of me being recognised there. After weighing the advantages and disadvantages I decided that on balance New Zealand was the safest option. I completed a final clean out of the house, finalised the tenancy with the landlord and completed all the last minute tasks. An acquaintance from work offered to drive me to Manchester airport in my car then sell it on my behalf after I left. I was grateful for his assistance and not really disappointed or surprised that the money from the sale of the car never arrived. At that time I had a sense of closure and incorrectly thought that I would never see England again.

8

The move to New Zealand

AUGUST 2002

I arrived jet lagged in Auckland, New Zealand and caught an airport coach directly to the eastern suburbs private hostel where I had pre-booked my accommodation over the internet. Although I was exhausted from travel, I didn't waste any time and within 48 hours of my arrival I had opened a bank account, deposited my cash reserves of a few thousand dollars, bought a mobile telephone and prepared a resume. Apart from the my telephone enquiries in response to jobs advertised in the local newspaper, during the next two weeks I sent out more than 40 written job applications for various jobs I felt confident I could bring value to.

By the end of the second week although I had been to several job interviews I still didn't have a job and was becoming a little desperate. I was relieved when I was offered an immediate interview with a scrap metal merchant on Saturday and was told the job was mine with a Monday morning start. It was a dirty and at times arduous job with very poor pay, but at last I had an income to support my week-to-week needs until I could find something better. I breathed a sigh of relief and decided to make the best of it.

For the first week I caught a bus to and from work each day. It was a 45 minute journey to work but the trip home varied between one and two hours depending on my quitting time and when the next bus was scheduled. The journey each way became an easy half-hour commute when I bought an old but tidy Toyota in the second week.

At work my primary task was to unload then weigh by metal type the various items of scrap metal that sellers bought to the yard on a huge set of scales before issuing them with payment dockets so that they could be paid at the cashiers window. The size and type of delivery varied from a single bag of aluminium cans to a full truckload of copper radiators that I needed to unload using a forklift truck.

Many of my customers were desperate individuals living on the edge of society. The same people would arrive each day in their old dilapidated, unregistered cars with $50 to $100 of scrap that they had found or stolen. Apart from government dole payments the sale of scrap was probably their only source of income and the difference of $10 either way in their daily transaction with me was often a survival issue for them. Many seemingly minor transactions were conducted in an atmosphere of high emotions. It could be quite unnerving.

During my second week with the scrap metal merchant I was invited back to a second interview with one of the companies that I had earlier applied to for work. The company had started life as a cleaning company and although that remained its core business, it had become an all trades property management business by adding additional trade services to its customers.

After the interview I was offered and accepted the job of a portfolio manager on the princely salary of $45,000 per year plus a company car and mobile telephone. It was a huge improvement on my personal income and employment conditions. When I gave one week's notice to my supervisor at the scrap metal merchant, he was most displeased that I was leaving and as a punishment for my ingratitude he allocated me some of the worst jobs he could think of.

On the second day of my notice I was allocated the task of feeding old alloy lawnmower bodies into a crunching machine that munched them up into small pieces that packed easily into bags for shipping to buyers. Although I kept my fingers well clear of the blade I was untrained and therefore unfamiliar with the characteristics of the machine. Within 10 minutes of starting one of the items I was feeding into the machine kicked violently downwards, catching my fingers between it and the machine. I couldn't see my fingers because I was wearing heavy leather gloves but I knew from the pain that this was a serious injury. I tentatively removed the glove off my right hand and found that the end of my forefinger had been chopped right off leaving the gruesome bone sticking out the end of it. The second finger had also been badly munched and was bleeding freely but seemed more or less intact.

I asked my supervisor to drive me to the nearest hospital but the foolish fellow felt duty bound to follow the company emergency procedure manual so he took me to the local medical centre instead. Finding no doctor on duty at that medical centre he consulted his manual and took me to another medical centre, where the duty doctor put on a rudimentary dressing before instructing him to take me to hospital with the amputated section of my finger in a jar filled with ice. At the hospital the paperwork seemed to take forever and for some reason all my clothing was removed, leaving me in a hospital gown with my bare bottom perilously exposed but at last, hours later, a doctor examined my hand. 'Ah!' he said knowingly. 'We will just take this forefinger finger off at the middle knuckle and the second finger off at the first knuckle.'

'No!' I replied with alarm. 'You mustn't do that. I have the missing section of my forefinger in that jar, you must put it all together again, and I certainly don't want anything cut off.' He sniffed impatiently as he removed and inspected the remains of my finger from the jar. 'No, that's just too damaged to do anything with,' he announced.

'It's best to just cut them off neat and tidy, they will heal very quickly and you will be back at work in two to three weeks at most, far more convenient all round.'

'Listen, you are not going to cut off my fingers!' I remonstrated angrily. 'I need microsurgery not butchery, I don't care about healing quickly. I am quite prepared for it to heal slowly and take longer to return to work. The critical issue is that you restore my fingers to as near to their original condition as you can. I can't grow new fingers.'

'I don't have time for this nonsense!' he replied haughtily. 'You just don't understand what is practical and what isn't. As it happens, I am trained to know'

'I do understand that I probably need to talk to a lawyer before we continue this conversation,' I replied quickly. 'I think I am in a first-world country but I really don't understand my rights. This is a very serious matter and I will need to take advice before we can proceed further.'

'Suit yourself!' he stammered before storming off with a small entourage of nurses and trainee doctors trailing behind him. In due course a nurse provided me with a cordless telephone and a set of the yellow pages. At random I selected one of the largest legal firms in Auckland from the yellow pages and after I was connected with a lawyer. He listened to all the details of my situation before undertaking to telephone me back within the hour.

When he did phone back he cheerfully announced that he had bad news, bad news, bad news and bad news. The first item of bad news was that the specific medical treatment I needed could not really be provided in a private hospital in Auckland, even if I could afford to pay for it, they really were not set up for that type of complex surgery. I was stuck with the surgical options offered by the public hospital system.

The second item of bad news is that no New Zealand employee is permitted to take legal action against an employer for workplace injuries no matter how negligent the employer may have been. A quasi government-owned Worker's Compensation Body funded the cost of all workplace injuries and they would only fund my treatment within the public health system. The third item of bad news was that during my period of recuperation I would be normally be compensated for lost income at a rate of 80 per cent of my previous month income. Since I had not been in the country earning income in the previous month, I would not be entitled to any compensatory income at all. It was therefore vital, the lawyer suggested, that I select the surgical option that offered a speedy return to work. The last item of bad news was that he was going to send me an invoice for $250 for his legal advice.

When at last the surgeon and his entourage returned to my bedside I was able to inform him: 'There are no viable options for me here. I am not going to let you cut off my fingers because it is convenient. Please apply a suitable dressing to my wounds, pack my section of amputated finger in fresh ice then discharge me. I will catch the first available flight back to Australia where there are proper doctors so that I can get proper medical treatment.'

The surgeon hesitated almost a minute before speaking. 'Let's be frank with one another sir. The amputated section of your finger really is far too damaged for any surgeon to reattach but there is a surgical procedure I can perform that will allow you to keep your fingers. I can cut some flesh out of your arm and use it to construct new fingertips then graft skin from your second finger to provide cover. I can do it! But you won't be able to work for months and after it is all healed you won't have any sensation in the fingertips. That lack of sensation will be a real nuisance in your work and home life, you will regret it. I strongly urge you to accept partial amputation but if you want your finger rebuilt, I can do it. What is it to be?'

'Please rebuild my fingers to as near original condition as you can with deference to form over function. I want them to look as normal as they can be,' I answered firmly.

'You will regret this, but it is your decision, I will do what you ask,' he said with a shake of his head. I gave a sigh of relief. I would work out later how to support myself in the post surgery period but in the meantime I had saved my fingers.

After the surgery, the nurse who changed my dressing indicated that the surgeon would probably look in on me tomorrow, but as far as she knew the operation had gone very well. She explained that in order to maintain blood flow to the skin graft on my first finger, the skin was still connected in a sheet from where it had been lifted from the second finger. And because it was all so fragile the first three fingers had all been sewn together to prevent movement. For the next few weeks my arm would need to stay elevated in a sling that was tethered above the bed. I had some pain but it was very little compared to the poor fellow in the next bed who had just had two of his fingers removed in one of the surgeon's easy and convenient operations.

'Without my obstinacy that could have been me, what a close run thing it had been,' I thought. I found my personal belongings including my wallet and a set of keys in the cabinet next to the bed but noted that my clothes were not only dirty from work duties they were also splattered with blood. In the late afternoon, as if visiting the toilet, still bare bottomed in my hospital gown I slipped quietly out of the ward, down the lift and caught a taxi in front of the hospital back to the hostel where I quickly packed three clean white shirts, underwear, socks, shoes and a suit into a bag. The round trip took almost two hours but I slipped back into the ward and stashed my bag in the storage cabinet before returning to bed without my absence being noticed by the nursing staff. I suppose they are used to smokers leaving the ward for a cigarette break.

The following morning after the nurse changed my dressing I shaved then washed myself in the bathroom as best I could before dressing myself in a crisp white shirt and tie with suit pants and shiny black dress shoes. After examining myself in the mirror I was satisfied that I was reasonably well turned out. I tethered my arm in the sling before sitting down on a chair next to the bed to wait for the surgeon. I was determined never again to be disadvantaged in my dealings with medical staff by interfacing with them as just another patient lying down in a bottomless hospital gown. I would meet them face to face, with dignity and require them to deal with me as an equal in every sense of the word. There was an immediate change in my working relationship with the nursing staff with my change of clothes. I had become a real person. The flow and quality of information regarding my prognosis and treatment significantly improved and I felt I had regained control of my destiny.

The surgeon seemed unsurprised that I was dressed and standing for his visit, perhaps the nursing staff had informed him.

'Well Rob, I have done what you wanted and it went as well as to be expected although you will never have any feeling in that forefinger. Why don't you go home tomorrow if you feel up to it and we will arrange for the district nurse to visit you each day to change your dressing? We will schedule you in for surgery in, say, two months to close off the skin graft and separate the fingers then we will start you on a program of physiotherapy to get everything working again. We could have you back at work on light duties as soon as mid January.'

Four days later with no sling and with my dressing stripped down to the absolute minimum I arrived on Monday morning to start my new job.

'I was attempting suicide due to my unsatisfactory romantic life but slit my finger instead of my wrist due to my poor cognitive ability. I am afraid it will take a few days to heal,' I explained to my new employer, who smiled as he accepted my condition, if not the explanation, without offering any comment.

My new job gave me four primary clients and managerial responsibility for about 50 part-time staff cleaning and undertaking other property management tasks in four shopping centres. Although it wasn't a difficult job I had staff working from 7.00am until midnight so it required me to work long days as well. I settled in and applied myself to the tasks at hand and to the best of my knowledge was well regarded by my clients and my employer. In late November I had the final surgical procedure to separate my fingers and by December I was able to stop applying dressings altogether.

It was also in November that I meet Marg who was to become my first real personal friend since I had been in Spain.

We wined and dined together before becoming romantically entangled. I am not well suited to a celibate, solitary life and it was almost a year since my last sexual interaction with Sheila so I didn't have a lot of resistance when the opportunity for intimacy presented itself, although I did have serious misgivings about the fact that Rob was not my real name. I thought it was ethically important to explain that I wasn't really who I appeared to be. 'I am obliged to tell you that I am in a witness protection program, Rob is not my real name!' I offered earnestly over dinner, expanding the explanation with untruthful detail.

'I am far more concerned about that awful red tie you are wearing than your name,' Marg replied cheerfully without any real interest in my story. We became sexually involved and in the weeks that followed we learned more about each other. I tried to be as truthful as I could, offering real anecdotes from my childhood, adolescence, marriage and past commercial life. I presented her with a reality of myself that was 90 per cent accurate. In the weeks that followed I learned about her childhood, life, children, failed marriage and discovered that the bank was about to foreclose on the rural smallholding that she and her husband had owned just out of Auckland, due to missed mortgage payments. Her personal financial situation was precarious. In January 2003 she sold her property and moved in with me into a small two-bedroom apartment I had rented in Auckland as much for practical financial reasons as for romance.

Although I had a good, secure, well-paid job, in December 2002 I decided that I would never be able to create personal wealth for myself as an employee of the property management company so I applied and was accepted for a selling position with Versatile Buildings Ltd. The self-employed position had no retainer and I needed to cover all of my own costs, but I was paid 5 per cent commission on everything I sold with no limit on my earnings.

It was exactly the type of position I needed to build wealth with skillful and diligent application. I was an immediate success and the manager at Versatile Buildings Ltd was very pleased with my sales performance. By February I had established and stabilised my income at more than double that it had been when I was an executive wage earner.

I had also slipped into an easy companionable life with Marg, living a good life with entertainment and eating out in fine restaurants regularly as my cash reserve continued to grow. Life was easy and kind to both of us, although on reflection I probably drank a little too much wine. Josaphine had not responded to any of my emails and by the middle of the year I assumed that she had stabilised herself into a new life in Australia and was cementing her relationship with her mother. 'Perhaps she will come to visit me with my grandson in a year or two,' I thought.

As my savings grew I started to plan new businesses that I could start or buy to start my last run as an entrepreneur in due course. Marg was easy to live with, nothing deep, but it could have lasted for several years and I reflected on what I would do if Sheila ever made contact with me and invited me back into her life. 'Who knows?' I thought.

Unexpectedly, in September 2003 there was a text message on my telephone from Josaphine asking me to telephone her on an English telephone number, my first contact with her in almost a year.

She explained that she was back in England teaching. Her relationships with her mother and her new stepfather, Bob, were a failure and she asked me to join up with her in England. Although I loved Josaphine it was most inconvenient to go to her and I didn't really want to give up the safe personal and commercial situation I had worked myself into. With a heavy heart I asked my supervisor for two weeks' vacation, knowing that I could stretch it into four or six weeks if needed. I moved my domestic household into a nice apartment, slightly cheaper and down market from Remuera, that I knew Marg could afford to pay herself if I didn't return, although I really hoped that I would. Perhaps Josaphine and Chriseb would be able to join me?

Marg had become very fond of me and unexpectedly was now tenaciously committed to our relationship. I was most untruthful and ridiculously disingenuous in explaining the details of my travel plans and future to her although the potential outcomes were basically correct. I told her that I was leaving to provide evidence on matters relating to my witness protection program and although I had high hopes of returning to her, there was every chance that the program would require me to remain overseas and that we may never see each other again. I released her from any obligation to me and suggested that if I did not return to her within a month, she should forget about me and get on with her life. She delivered me to the airport for a tearful farewell and it really would have better served both of our interests if we had never met again. It wasn't that easy, and she was keen to maintain email contact with me and attempted to keep the relationship going in the months that followed.

9

Back to England

After another grinding aeroplane trip to England followed by a train trip then a cab ride, I found my way to Josaphine's quaint little home and let myself in with the key she had posted to me. Josaphine was teaching at a large high school in the city of Tamworth in the North of England, but lived in the pretty little village of Measham, about 15 minutes drive out of Tamworth.

In the next few days during many hours of conversation I learned more about the last year she had spent in Australia and her motivation for returning to England. 'It was awful Daddy' she explained sadly. 'When we arrived I found that Mum and Bob are living together as a couple in our home. It isn't our home anymore. She made it clear that my bedroom was now their guest room and she had even moved all my clothes and stuff up to North Arm Cove. It was as if I had never lived there. She told me that I could live up at North Arm Cove rent free until I got on my feet but that was all. I didn't have any money, I couldn't get a job up there, I was just so isolated and on my own. It was a really hard year!'

'Why didn't you let me know what was happening?' Why didn't you respond to any of my emails?' I asked curiously.

'I misplaced your email address in the move to Australia Daddy. I had your mobile telephone number stored on my English mobile phone but I didn't feel it was safe to activate that phone in Australia to call you. The whole purpose of you being in a witness protection program is to keep you safe,' she replied, explaining the mystery of why she had not contacted me for a year.

'What about your relationship with your mother?' I asked. 'I know that she has moved on from me with her new husband but did you manage to establish some sort of emotional bond with her? Have you made any progress at all?'

'Emotional bond!' she spluttered. 'They were both awful and I don't think we met more than 12 times in the whole year and when I did see them they were both so coarse with me and each other it was just awful. She and Bob are both absorbed in their little life together and I don't fit into it. The whole point of me going back to Australia was to make that relationship work. Well! I can tell you now it will never happen.'

'So why leave Australia and come back to England rather than just relocate to Sydney or some other area where there was work?' I asked.

'I needed to make contact with you and I didn't feel safe turning on the mobile telephone until I left Australia. I didn't know where you were, but I knew as soon as I made contact with you that you would find your way to me. Even if I did turn on the phone in Australia I knew we could never have meaningful contact until I left Australia, you could never visit me there,' she replied quickly.

'Anyway, there was no point in staying in Australia! I couldn't meet the primary objective you set for me of securing my inheritance by improving the relationship with Mum. It was easy for me to get a job back here in England and childcare is affordable so I am self supporting. I knew you would come as long as I could establish a base here in England and make contact with you. We will have to force her to sell the family assets and give us our half,' she said as she screwed up her face.

'She is coming over to visit us at Christmas. She told me she plans to visit me once every year. It's to keep up appearances with her family and has nothing to do with wanting to see me. Force her to give up our share of the assets and then we can just cut her loose from our lives for once and for all,' she concluded bitterly. Although Josaphine was angry with her mother, beneath that I could see that she was deeply hurt. Sheila had not only abandoned me she had, for all intents and purposes, given up on her daughter and grandson too.

I briefed Josaphine on the details of my life in New Zealand over the past year, including the injury to my fingers, my commercial life then reluctantly told her about my romantic life with Marg with more than a little embarrassment. 'Daddy has a girlfriend! Daddy has a sex life!' she sang with a little dance to accompany it for good measure, obviously not damaged or upset with the information. After some discussion we agreed it was in our best financial interest for me to return to New Zealand and continue my commercial life at Versatile Buildings Ltd for the next two months then return again at Christmas when Sheila came to England. After Sheila's visit we would decide if I should remain in England with Josaphine and Chriseb or whether they should come to New Zealand with me. It all depended on the outcome of our meeting with Sheila.

I think it was John Lennon who said that life is what happens when you are making other plans, and isn't that the truth. Just when I least expected it I suffered another series of minor strokes, there was no mistaking it with heatstroke this time and thank goodness Josaphine was right there on hand to help me this time.

'Don't you damn well die on me Daddy,' she shouted as she rushed me to hospital, driving at breakneck speed. 'If you don't slow down you are going to kill us all,' I wanted to say. But I couldn't form the words as I had lost the ability to speak. I noted with embarrassment that I had urinated in my pants. I had no feeling in one leg but the other leg was very wet. 'Surely they will understand that I am not the sort of chap who normally urinates in my pants,' I hoped.

Josaphine was cool under pressure and had me admitted to hospital under my false name without any difficulty. She probably saved my life that night. After my last hospital experience in New Zealand when my fingers had been injured, I was surprised at how little is actually done in hospital for someone who has suffered a stroke. Apart from the chemical intervention of the medication there is little they could do for me except monitor my condition. I don't know what I had expected? Within days I was back home with Josaphine and attending outpatient recuperative physiotherapy three times a week. My physical condition appeared to return to normality far more quickly than my mental ability. 'I don't know how I will ever be able to work again?' I bemoaned to Josaphine. 'I can't remember things. Whole sections of my memory and cognitive ability have gone.'

'Daddy, you weren't that flash to begin with, you always

survived on a cunning turn of phrase and your big brown eyes, you were never a great intellectual!' she informed me cheerfully. Although I was now a functioning human again, it was clear that I wouldn't be returning to New Zealand before Christmas if ever.

Josaphine terminated Chriseb's daycare arrangements so that I could become his full-time carer while she was at work, correctly understanding that it would be good for both Chriseb and me. I enrolled him in the local village kindergarten for a couple of half day sessions each week so that he would continue to have interaction with other children. I also enrolled him in a physical activity group called Tumble Tots for two sessions a week in the village hall that required my involvement with him as he participated in various physical learning activities. The Tumble Tots sessions probably aided my recovery from the strokes more than any of the physiotherapy. I held his little hand as he learned to walk along a plank, encouraged him to crawl through the tunnels and assisted him as he learned to tumble on the mat and much, much more.

Each day after we had completed our activity we walked to the village bakery and bought a treat for him before stopping at the butcher and grocer to buy our ingredients for the evening dinner I would prepare for us all later. We read stories together at home, played in the park together and often stopped at the local pub where he would have a glass of lemonade as I had a beer. We bonded again and became very tight with one another.

On reflection it was probably one of the most meaningful and enjoyable periods of my life. There was an internet facility in the public library of the next village that was a 45-minute walk away from home. Chriseb and I walked there once a week. Using the paperwork I had brought with me from New Zealand I was able to file my bimonthly GST tax returns and pay the tax on line by transferring money from my New Zealand bank account directly to the tax department. I also informed Versatile Buildings Ltd that I had suffered a stroke with my prognosis and return date to New Zealand left as uncertain. My contact with Marg in New Zealand was far more complicated. Upon learning about my stroke she wanted to fly to England to be with me and was most forceful in her insistence that the relationship should continue. Although she had very limited financial reserves she was and is a resourceful woman and I was alarmed that if she made specific inquiries with the Australian embassy my whole imaginary life as Rob would unravel and become exposed. Although she didn't know exactly who I was, she knew enough to connect the dots if she really put her mind to it.

I considered telling her that I just didn't want her in my life anymore. That was the simplest and kindest solution but in the time I had been living with her I had learned of some alarming acts of revenge she had taken against her ex-husband as a woman scorned after he had terminated their marriage.

So instead of telling her in a straightforward way that I needed her to be out of my life, I told her more lies and gave her undertakings that I would maintain contact and return to her if I could.

Josaphine and I discussed how we would handle the meetings with Sheila when she visited and concluded that it probably didn't serve our best interests for me to have face to face meetings with her. Although my mental condition had significantly improved since my stroke I was still obviously damaged and the cognition problems lingered. It often took a few minutes for me to be able to grasp a simple concept outside the normal everyday routine.

We agreed that we would not tell Sheila about the stroke as we were worried that at the slightest sign of weakness Sheila would exploit her advantage over me. We decided that I should move into a hotel for the period of her visit and Josaphine would shuttle correspondence between us every couple of days. Sheila responded angrily to my letters.

'What right have you got to get involved in our lives?' she demanded. 'I have sold Josaphine's Sydney investment flat and her car for her and deposited the proceeds into her bank account; she has almost A$100,000. She doesn't need any of my money and you certainly don't have any right to anything.'

Slowly, over a period of days she conceded that I did have some property rights but paying me out created too much of a security risk for her. After lengthy and torturous negotiation she ultimately agreed that she would pay A$250,000 into a Swiss bank account that Josaphine already had once a year every year for the next four years. It was to be a simple one million dollar settlement spread over the next four years with the first payment due on or before Christmas in December 2004.

Although there was very little prospect of AMP ever settling the insurance claim of $3.5 million, she agreed that if they did she would pay me an additional one million dollars in two equal payments of $500,000 over two years. At last it was settled between us with firm arrangements and dates. On 4 January 2004, Josaphine delivered Sheila to the airport and I was able to move back into the village home with them.

In the following days we discussed our living arrangements many times and agreed that for the next year, as we waited for our first payment we should all live in New Zealand. Josaphine would quarantine A$30,000 into the special European emergency bank account in case anything went wrong and I would return to New Zealand by myself at the end of February, taking A$30,000 of her money back with me to add to my reserves and assist with set up costs. I would find and rent a suitable home so that Josaphine and Chriseb could join me in early April.

Just before Sheila's arrival, our lives had taken on an unexpected but most welcome complication in December, when Josaphine immersed herself in an unplanned romance with a local Englishman after meeting him at a pre-Christmas party. This was her first romance since she had left Pete almost 20 months earlier and a welcome development in her emotional life. Although I missed her company when she was out and about I was very happy for her. Chriseb and I developed new routines, often rushing to have a quick early supper with Josaphine as soon as she returned from work then waving her goodbye before spending the evenings at home by ourselves as she went out with the new man in her life. 'This will end in tears when you have to leave for New Zealand in April!' I chided her gently.

'I know that Daddy,' she said. 'But I am going to make hay while the sun shines. Who knows when I will have romance again?' she replied earnestly. In early January there was a cold snap and our village, like most of Northern England, was covered in a blanket of snow. Chriseb and I built a snowman together and I towed him about the village on an improvised sled we made out of a toy box lid. It was one of many delightful experiences we shared and was made all the more joyful by the knowledge that he and Josaphine would be joining me in New Zealand.

10

Return to New Zealand

MARCH 2004

I arrived back in New Zealand on 2 March 2004 and moved back into the private hostel I had lived in before. From the emails I had received from Marg, I knew that she had sold my elderly Toyota so I bought a little red Audi to replace it and set about putting my life back together.

I emailed the Auckland manager of Versatile Buildings Ltd explaining that I was back in New Zealand, 85 per cent recovered from my stroke and seeking a selling position again if he had a vacancy and would like to consider me. He replied that he was interested and arranged for me to call on him on 9 March.

It all seemed to be coming together easily when I received a message at the hostel that Marg had called looking for me. With Josaphine and Chriseb arriving shortly I really did have to finish with her but I had hoped to get a little more settled before I had to face her. I didn't have a plan to manage her and knew I would just have to face it. At least now that I was back she wouldn't be making any enquiries about who I really was and where I was. If she wanted she could just turn up and throw rocks at me. I could handle that, after 25 years of marriage with Sheila I was well trained to absorb anger.

'We had a great time together,' I told her when we met. 'It's not that I don't care for you, it's just that my daughter and grandson are coming to live with me, my priorities have changed, and I am marching to the beat of a different drum. I hope we will remain friends but there is no room for romance in my life, not with you, not with anyone!' She reluctantly conceded that the romance was over. 'Well, let's just be friends then!' she concluded sadly.

I rented a large three-bedroom house in the suburb of St Johns and filled it with functional, plain furniture then I bought a second hand BMW for Josaphine to drive. I found a small yacht that needed refurbishment at the bargain price of $6,500. The yacht was in very poor condition but it came with a mooring at Okahu Bay that was only 10 minutes drive from our rented home so I snapped it up.

'Fixing it up and painting it will be an excellent project for Josaphine,' I thought as I sat in the boat's cockpit inspecting the peeling paint. My meeting with the manager at Versatile Buildings Ltd went well. I was not just welcomed back but also invited to change from selling their garages and small buildings to selling their range of homes. I was allocated sole selling rights for their homes in the territory of the West and North of Auckland. Although the sales and consent process was more complicated, selling houses was far more lucrative and I was paid a significant fee for drawing up plans and obtaining local body consent in addition to my sales commission. My total average income per sale was to be about $4,000 and there was an expectation that I would sell approximately four homes each month. I was delighted with the arrangement and settled happily into my new office.

Josaphine and Chriseb arrived on 1 April and after a happy reunion we very quickly settled into a comfortable domestic routine that included sailing in our yacht almost every Sunday followed by dinner and drinks at the yacht club.

Although there were no significant problems in our life, we had enough money and a plan for the future I noticed sadness in Josaphine and she was drinking too much wine with her dinner each night. 'What's the problem kiddo?' I inquired. 'I don't know what is troubling you but whatever it is we had better fix it!'

In the conversation that followed I learned that she was heartsick about giving up her romantic life with the English chap she had left behind.

'He is not the sort of person you would pick for me because he is a bit of a rough diamond but he is a good man. I love him and miss him Daddy and want to go back to have my life with him. What if he is my true love, my one real chance at happiness and I have just walked away?'

'If he is that important to you perhaps you need to go back and make your life with him,' I said. 'You can return to your teaching work in England and I will remain here in New Zealand this year until your mother pays us the first payment. Hopefully next year I can buy a pub in England and we can link up again. Apart from the money she pays us I plan to have a good financial year here and I may be able to save another A$50,000. If I sell our assets in an orderly manner when I leave, we shouldn't lose too much on them so perhaps this time next year we will have about A$350,000 deposit for a rundown pub with the next payment of A$250,000 due by the following Christmas. We can make this work kiddo, if you have found true love you need to grab it!'

141

In the following weeks Josaphine made her arrangements with the chap in England and flew out on 28 May. Our time together in New Zealand had lasted less than two months and although I dearly loved my daughter, parting with my grandson Chriseb was the most heart wrenching.

In early June I bought a little home not far from the home we had been renting and moved in. Although Josaphine and Chriseb were living in England it would be a family home if they came to visit and I felt confident that I would be able to improve it and sell it at a profit when the time came for me to move to England. June was an extraordinarily busy and lucrative month for me in my work with Versatile Buildings Ltd. There was a planned change in local body legislation that would significantly increase the building permit fees on 1 July, so many of my clients were anxious to finalise their contracts with me on the condition that I would lodge their building application with the relevant local body by 30 June. I sold 13 homes that month, the equivalent of three months' normal sales and I lodged all the applications into councils by the due date. It was an all time record for Versatile Buildings Ltd in West Auckland, a huge effort for me but the remuneration gave me a solid financial base and a whole new level of security.

I had received the occasional friendly phone call from Marg in the previous couple of months and after Josaphine and Chriseb left she visited me at my office in early June.

'Gosh Rob, you have obviously hit your stride, haven't you?' she said when she learned how busy I was, working 14 hours a day, seven days a week with an overload of new sales and plan drawing work. 'How about giving me a part time job?' she inquired. 'You obviously need some help and I could use some extra income.'

We agreed on a $100 per day fee for five hours work each

Sunday and although her input was limited, it was very helpful to have her assistance. After work on Sunday nights we often shared a bottle of wine with a take out dinner at the office and during the week she invited me to call and have dinner at her home on my way home. Because of my workload I often didn't arrive until 9.30 at night but she didn't seem to mind. Although she applied a little pressure and tension from time to time for the relationship to return to a romantic partnership, for the most part our relationship was easygoing and friendly. She had started to date other men and often gave me a humorous update of her latest romantic encounter.

Josaphine and Chriseb returned to New Zealand from England quickly and unexpectedly in mid-August. Josaphine was distraught. 'The whole thing was a disaster Daddy!' she snorted. 'Before I left he had told me that he would make all the domestic arrangements before I arrived, house car, everything would be waiting for us. He said he had a great job, I could work if I wanted to but there was really no need.'

She paused then continued. 'There was nothing Daddy, it was all lies, we had to stay in a hotel until I could find and rent a place, then I had to buy another house load of furniture, a car, everything!' She paused, shaking her head. 'You really don't know somebody until you live with them do you?'

'But what about your romantic relationship with him?' I asked. 'What about true love, where are you with all that?'

'I am heartbroken Daddy. He is a lovely man, lots of fun to be with, romantic and kind but he is a complete disaster. After I got over the initial shock of funding all the set-up costs I assumed it would all come together for us. I was starting to get some casual teaching work and he had a good full-time job. Just when it seemed to becoming right he would do something strange like spending all of his pay on expensive toys for Chriseb

143

and gifts for me so that there was nothing for rent or food. He had a heart of gold but no concept of responsibility at all. I was going through my savings like water, the whole exercise cost A\$30,000 and I would have gone broke if I didn't leave when I did,' she said sadly.

So they were home, damaged and poorer, but we were a family again. We arranged daycare for Chriseb and had the yacht pulled out of the water onto a hardstand at Okahu Bay boatyard for Josaphine to repair and paint as her personal project.

Josaphine seemed keen enough to get on with the project but her ability to work was limited by very poor weather and she made very little progress. She was obviously hurt by the broken relationship with the English chap and during rainy periods for light relief she enjoyed socialising with some of the men working on boats at the boatyard and even went out several times for a drink at the pub in the evening with a group of them. Although the social interaction was initially harmless, her choice of company was ill-considered and she developed a light romance with one of them. The romance and some of her decisions during that time indicated substantial lapses of judgment during a time when she seemed to lose her inner compass. The yacht project dragged on far longer than we had allowed. Finally, in late October although the hull and other critical items had been repaired and painted we put the yacht back into the water with much of the finishing work incomplete. During this time my work selling houses for Versatile Buildings Ltd continued successfully but I gave up working Sundays, devoting the day entirely to adventures with my grandson Chriseb. We spent days at the beach and flew a kite in the park but our most regular excursion was swimming together in the hot pools at Parakai.

One afternoon when Chriseb and I were driving back from the Parakai Hot Pool, Marg telephoned and asked us to collect her from Auckland Hospital and drive her home. She had been on a romantic weekend with her latest lover on his boat in a bay about an hour north of Auckland when she had dislocated her arm as she stepped awkwardly into a dinghy. Her new romantic friend had called emergency services and in a flurry of drama a helicopter had flown her down to Auckland Hospital for treatment but she had left her handbag on the boat so she was stranded at the hospital without money. 'Why didn't the new man in your life rush down to be at your bedside?' I asked cheerfully.

'I think all the fuss might have put him off,' she chortled. We took her home, made her dinner and gave her some money to tide her over until she recovered her handbag. It was Chriseb's first real interaction with Marg and they enjoyed each other's company. Marg later babysat Chriseb for me from time to time whenever I had a late sales call to make and Josaphine wasn't available.

In November we moved Chriseb to a different daycare facility called McDonald's Farm. It was associated with a pet animal tourist farm in a semi-rural area only 10-minutes' drive from my office and the children interacted with the animals every day as part of their normal day. Our domestic routine changed also. Now, after breakfast every morning, Chriseb and I would drive to his daycare for an 8.00am start and I would collect him at 4.45pm each day. We ate ice cream each day on the drive home together and often cooked dinner together if Josaphine was out on a date. For a little while, during this difficult time for her, although she was never neglectful of Chriseb's needs or mine, Josaphine spent a great deal of time away from home involved in her romantic life. In early 2005 her relationship with the fellow she had become involved with at the boatyard ended, and she seemed to find her equilibrium again.

In early 2005 I had a couple of brief telephone conversations with Sheila about the A$250,000 payment that she was overdue in making to us. Sheila indicated that there would have to be a delay of several months and that it would be necessary for Josaphine to spend a little time in Australia. She said that although there was no prospect of AMP ever paying the A$3,500,000 life insurance claim, they required statements from both her and Josaphine to close their file and may consider making a small settlement payment at some later date.

Both the delay and Josaphine's time in Australia seemed reasonable if Sheila was in a new period of investigation so after making the necessary arrangements both Josaphine and Chriseb travelled to Australia and stayed at our North Arm Cove home. Not long after their arrival Josaphine telephoned me from a call box to tell me that they would need to change the plan. 'We can't stay here Daddy. Chriseb talks all the time about his grandpa in New Zealand, and as soon as we meet anyone in the family they will know within a few minutes that you are alive and living in New Zealand.'

We arranged for them both to return to New Zealand on 19 February and after spending the weekend together Josaphine travelled back to Australia by herself on 23 February leaving Chriseb with me. Chriseb and I returned to our former domestic routine together with me dropping him off and picking him up from McDonald's Farm daycare each day. I hired Marg to babysit Chriseb on Saturdays when I was working, then Chriseb and I would spend Sunday together on some sort of an excursion. After another three weeks away, Josaphine completed her interview with the AMP investigators and returned to New Zealand on 13 March.

'How did it go?' I asked.

'The whole thing was awful Daddy,' she replied sourly. 'I had to confirm the same basic information I had supplied at the coroner's court when I really did believe you were dead. I am sorry if you were hoping that they still may pay Mum something because they will never pay anything after meeting with me. I not only avoided answering a lot of their questions, I had to refuse to sign their record of interview. I'm really sorry Daddy if that mucks something up with you and Mum but I just couldn't sign off on a false statement, it would have been fraud. You didn't want me to get involved in that did you?'

'You did exactly the right thing!' I replied happily. 'I don't care if they never pay your mother anything, we would never see any of the money anyway. We just want our share of the assets, to stay out of jail, to go to England and buy a pub. We just want to get on with our lives don't we?' We all settled down into a domestic routine together again.

Just before she had left for New Zealand Josaphine had met and been on a couple of dates with a new fellow. He didn't appear to have any assets or even own a car but he was a nice enough chap and a welcome relief after her last disastrous romantic relationship.

When she returned from New Zealand she rekindled her romance with him and it seemed to be a far healthier relationship than the last one. I don't know if she fell in love with him but she seemed quite keen to have him in her life and even talked of inviting him to join us in England if and when we relocated. We were growing less and less confident that Sheila would honour her agreement to make the four payments of A$250,000 without additional pressure and resolved to give her an absolute drop-dead deadline of Christmas 2005, one year later, to make the first payment.

11

Meeting my new wife

DECEMBER 2004

My own romantic life had changed also. Just before Christmas of 2004, amongst the many prospective clients who called at the Versatile Buildings yard to inspect the show homes, a special lady had captured my interest at a very personal level. Although I suppose she is an ordinary person, it seemed that she was sprinkled with magic fairy dust and I became smitten with her. Everything she said seemed to be the most interesting thing I had ever heard and I was also attracted to her in a very physical way.

We had several commercial meetings in the following months at the show homes and at potential sites she was considering buying, but although our relationship was friendly it was never anything other than professional. Our last commercial meeting was at a property she had bought and was now living in. At her request I presented her with a formal quotation to build an additional home on the front of this new property. As we discussed the quotation I noticed two photos on her wall of ornate doors. I recognised them immediately as being doors of hotels in Tossa de Mar in Spain and after asking about them she told me that she had photographed them during a holiday there in 2001, the same time when I had been in Spain. Our conversation became personal and we shared our thoughts and feelings on a range of life issues. Our conversation lasted more than an hour and she noticed that she was late for an Eco Show, hosted by the local council that she intended to attend that day. Without ceremony she invited me to join her for the outing at the show.

'Don't do this. No matter how much you like her remember that she is a real person and you are an imaginary person,' I told myself before gently declining the invitation.

In the following week I daydreamed about her constantly and convinced myself there was no harm in inviting her to share a visit to the art gallery with me. We both shared a very keen interest in art and some of our previous personal conversation related to the Auckland Art Gallery. 'Perhaps we can just be platonic friends.' I suggested to myself as I picked up the telephone and asked her out. The Art Gallery outing led to her inviting me to her official housewarming party, then I invited her and one of her grandchildren to join Chriseb and me for an outing at the zoo telling myself: 'This is nothing serious, we are just two grandparents sharing a day out at the zoo with our grandchildren.' Of course it was serious and with each additional meeting we became closer and closer until I was totally in love with her. 'I don't know what the hell I am doing with this Kristine woman?' I told Josaphine. 'She isn't a casual person and this isn't a casual love affair. If I continue the relationship with her I will want and need her to marry me. She isn't a girlfriend sort of a person. It isn't like that at all. You know as well as I do that I am an imaginary person, I am not free to marry anybody, what the hell am I doing?'

'Daddy if you love her, don't you dare let her go. Harry Gordon doesn't exist anymore. Harry Gordon is dead and a death certificate has been issued. To the best of my knowledge Mum is either already married or planning to marry Bob. You were given your new identity by a formal witness protection program, you now really are Rob and you are not married to anyone else, you are free. Marry her Daddy, don't let love pass you by. This is too important,' she replied enthusiastically.

'What about buying a pub in England? She has children and grandchildren here in Auckland. She would never relocate to England,' I replied defensively, all too aware that the witness protection program I was in was anything but formal.

'Daddy we will work it out and it will be all right. Perhaps she will marry you, perhaps she won't, perhaps you can persuade her to come to England, perhaps not, perhaps we need to spend part of the year in England and part here, perhaps we all have to live our lives here in New Zealand. Whatever we need to do, it will be all right with me. We will work it out. Don't let love pass you by Daddy, it won't come again. Haven't you always told me that life is about relationships, not geography?'

'It's wrong Josaphine, I shouldn't even be thinking about continuing the relationship with her. I am not real. Her whole perception of who I am is based on a pack of lies.'

'Wake up to yourself Daddy! The background details of your life don't matter, they never have and never will. How you are is what matters and you are exactly how you seem to be. You are a person of good character, a man of substance and she is lucky to have you,' she concluded forcefully.

Although I should have known better, I threw caution to the wind and the relationship blossomed. I told Kristine my real name and informed her that I had become Rob in a witness protection program. I told her that I loved her and wanted to spend the rest of my life with her and we set 7 September as our date to be married.

In mid-May Kristine drove down to the east coast city of Tauranga to visit some of her old friends. We arranged for me to fly down to Tauranga on Sunday morning to spend Sunday with her and her friends before we drove back together on Sunday night. As part of Sunday outing together we took a leisurely stroll around the walking track at Mount Maunganui and as we walked, to my horror, I noticed my brother and his wife walking on the same track the other way so that they could clearly see my features. I walked past them hoping that they would allow the encounter to pass without making contact but it wasn't to be, after a few paces they doubled back and my brother said: 'Hello! Is that really you?'

I confirmed that it was indeed me but this was an inappropriate time for conversation and made a commitment to telephone him within a few days. I later offered an explanation to Kristine that they were some old friends from my previous commercial life. I telephoned my brother the following week and met him in late May then later again in late June. He seemed pleased that I was still alive and we loosely discussed the reasons for my disappearance and my plans for the future.

At his request I consented to him informing our sister True that I was still alive and after making telephone contact with me she flew to Auckland to meet with me. On the basis of family confidentiality, I spoke with them in a quite uninhibited way about my past problems, my fears and fantasies and my plans for the future, both real and imagined. It was wonderful to have contact with them again but both they and I knew that their lives could not really intersect with the imaginary life I was living and ongoing contact with them was minimal. I was not at all concerned that contact with them may have any adverse impact on my personal security as they were my family and it was unimaginable to me that they would betray me.

I was quite unaware that following my contact with her, my sister informed Sheila that she knew I was still alive and arranged a meeting with her. Evidently, both my brother and my sister attended the meeting with Sheila and advised her that her best course of action was to contact the police and make a statement informing them that I was still alive. There was no suggestion from any of them that Sheila and I should jointly seek legal advice before going to the police together. They decided it was in Sheila's best interest to get in first by herself and offer me up to the police. Evidently acting on their advice Sheila did in fact make contact with the NSW Police on 15 August, not only letting them know I was alive but advising them of my home and office addresses.

Josaphine and I were blissfully unaware of the betrayal by my siblings, nor the ambush Sheila had arranged with the police. However, we were both concerned that despite my excellent income, our cash reserves had been really run down for a number of reasons. As Kristine's fiancé I was no longer living a frugal lifestyle and had spent thousands of dollars on jewellery plus other gifts of love. As is so often the case during a romance, I was also spending much more than normal time each month on courtship rituals with the added impact of a reduced income as I worked fewer hours to devote more time to my emotional life. I expected this cash flow shortfall would stabilise in due course, after my marriage, but it was quite disconcerting in the short term to be spending more than I was earning.

I had now moved in with Kristine and was, quite properly, sharing the costs of her household while I continued to carry approximately $3,500 per month of costs to support Josaphine and Chriseb household.

Despite the fact that Chriseb had been in full-time daycare for a variety of very valid reasons Josaphine hadn't worked for more than a year. She too had some spending issues. She had spent more than $30,000 on the failed English romance and an unknown amount on her rebound romance with the predatory fellow from the boatyard.

Although refurbishing of the yacht had not been completed that project had turned out to be unexpectedly expensive. Josaphine had also carried significant travel, living and legal costs relating to her recent trips to Australia both with and without Chriseb. Josaphine briefly considered securing a local teaching job and continuing to live in our home in St Johns but discarded the concept as financially unworkable. Her latest romance had just about run its course. He had moved in with her and had become an additional overhead for her to carry.

'I don't think I can manage here financially Daddy,' she said. 'The mortgage, electricity and rates are about $1,800 per month. I will need another $650 a month for Chriseb's daycare plus, say, another $1,500 per month to run the car and buy groceries, clothes, etc. That's $4,000 a month! The most I can hope to earn after tax as a teacher here is $2,600 per month. The arithmetic just doesn't add up.'

'Well, I can subsidise you,' I offered. 'What if I helped with a $1,000 a month and you got the same from your boyfriend. Surely he can't expect to live here with you rent free?'

'Nah, I don't think so Daddy,' she replied as she wrinkled her forehead. 'He isn't part of any solution. It's time I gave him the flick and I need to be self supporting again. I don't want you propping me up. I have been looking at jobs with overseas schools and think I may take a one-year posting at an international school in Brunei. The pay isn't that great but I can be self supporting because an apartment is supplied and the living costs are cheap but more importantly Chriseb can attend their kindergarten free of charge. The financial arithmetic would work for me. What say I spend a year there? That will give you time and elbow room to settle into your new marriage before you chase up Mum for the overdue payment. Let's review in a year?'

'I don't want to be apart from you and Chriseb for a year,' I replied sadly.

'We can visit you during the year. We will fly down and visit you once or twice and you can visit us. Brunei isn't that far away and travel isn't that expensive, there are often excellent special airline deals to Malaysia. But apart from all that Daddy, you will have a new wife, you need some time alone to settle in as a couple and find your feet,' she replied finally.

It was settled and they flew out in early August leaving a huge gap in my emotional life despite having Kristine.

12

The beginning of the end

AUGUST 2005

August 2005 was an unusual and very busy month for me. Josaphine was involved in a traffic accident a few days before she left New Zealand so her BMW car was inconveniently left in a smash repair shop. I had to arrange all the insurance documents, pay the significant excess costs plus some non-insured repairs then collect then and store the car after she left. Her live-in boyfriend planned to return to Australia to live with his parents in Brisbane after Josaphine left. But he was not ready to vacate our St Johns house for the couple of weeks it took him to give notice and get ready to leave New Zealand. Although he didn't damage the house in any way, like a 40-year old teenager, he didn't clean or tidy anything either. After he left I needed to sort and empty the contents before spring cleaning the whole place.

On Monday 22 August I went into my office at Versatile Buildings Ltd and found that over the weekend it had been broken into and burgled. The policeman who inspected the scene found it very odd that although there were several other offices and of course the show homes that were filled with valuables, only my office had been burgled and all the missing items were personal. My laptop computer and diary were missing from my desk and a couple of carry bags with personal documents were missing.

In the documents that had gone missing were all the bank and credit card numbers as well as pin numbers for EFTPOS access. I quickly contacted the bank and the numbers were changed without any losses, but I had forgotten that the details about access for Josaphine's emergency bank account in Europe were also there. Without our knowledge almost the entire A$30,000 fund was siphoned off within days. Even if I had known, I had no way of contacting Josaphine at that time to arrange for her to place a hold on the account.

Two days later my difficulties increased with a workplace injury when, as was my habit I arrived at work a little before 7.00am. Versatile Buildings Ltd had engaged some construction contractors to erect additional new show buildings in the rear of our yard and one of the carpenters had strung an electrical cord at shin height across the pathway I needed to walk along in order to reach the rear door of the office to open up.

I was in brisk mid-stride that morning when the wire caught my shin and I fell heavily across some of the builder's debris beside the pathway. With my back wrenched out of place I was unable to move so I called an ambulance on my mobile telephone and was taken to hospital in great pain. I was released from hospital later that evening but could barely move. I was unable to walk properly for days, so Kristine and I discussed the possibility that we would need to postpone our wedding. Although I continued to suffer significant back pain and was unable to return to work within a few days I regained enough mobility to get myself up and around the house and for us to proceed with the wedding, notwithstanding the potential honeymoon limitations. Although I had not forgotten about the burglary, my focus had naturally shifted to my injury and the forthcoming wedding so I didn't reflect enough on what all the implications of the burglary might be. It was an expensive oversight.

On 7 September in a small ceremony and reception for less than 30 of Kristine's family and friends, we were married at the Hunting Lodge in Waimauku. Despite my back injury we had a wonderful, loving almost dreamlike honeymoon in Raratonga where we enjoyed each other, the sunshine, the holiday and the sense that we were a couple. It really seemed to be a new beginning, but our sense of wellbeing came to an abrupt end as we attempted to board the aeroplane early on 18 September back to New Zealand from Raratonga.

My Rob passport had been flagged as stolen by the Australian Police and that information came up on the Air New Zealand computer. As well as being denied access onto the aeroplane, the airline staff confiscated my passport. Although I was still unaware of my betrayal by my siblings and Sheila's ambush I now formed the view that the passport problem and the burglary were probably connected and my imaginary life was becoming unravelled.

I briefly convinced Kristine that she should return to New Zealand and she boarded the aeroplane without me. After an emotional outburst she asked and was permitted to disembark from the aeroplane. Although I was not able to find a way to get myself on the plane, I managed to persuade the airline staff to return my Rob passport to me.

'I don't see how you have a lawful right to hold it?' I told them. 'You are not a law enforcement agency. If the Australian immigration doesn't believe I am entitled to it why haven't they asked the Raratonga Immigration Department or the police to take it from me?' I demanded and they lost their nerve and gave it back. Later the same day I convinced my very unhappy bride to return to New Zealand on the evening flight without me.

The following day I investigated all my alternative options for leaving Raratonga, including a berth on a yacht that was available, but finally settled on flying to Fiji. I correctly guessed that Fiji's immigration department would not have their computer linked to Australia or New Zealand, and that they would accept my Rob passport at face value. I bought a ticket to Fiji and flew into Nandi, where as I guessed there were no questions about my passport.

After my arrival in Fiji I considered all of my options for further travel. I still had some money and the financial capacity to fly from Fiji to Korea, then on to Malaysia before linking up with Josaphine in Brunei. Seductive as that option was, with continuing freedom, I also understood that I now had significant ethical obligations relating to my marriage to Kristine. It would just be unconscionable to abandon her without an explanation. It was clear to me that whatever the cost I had to return to Kristine. I didn't know for sure what the police knew or didn't know, I just knew it was all unravelling and it was time sort it out. My time as Rob was over.

As I was still unaware that Rob himself had betrayed me, and that he was part of the reason the police were onto me, I telephoned my brother in New Zealand and asked him to collect a document box from my office at Versatile Buildings, locate my old Harry Gordon birth certificate and an old expired Harry Gordon Australian passport in it and send them by courier to me at Nandi airport. He said he was happy to do so.

After several anxious days in Nandi the documents finally arrived and I travelled to the capital city of Suva and presented myself at the passport office of the New Zealand embassy.

'I have lost my passport!' I told the woman. 'I have sailed into Fiji as part of the regatta and think I left my bag with the passport on the last yacht I was on. It is no longer in port and I think they were headed to Hawaii. I have contacted my brother in New Zealand and he has sent me my birth certificate by courier, what should I do next?'

On the woman's instructions I went down to the central Fiji police station where I reported the loss and a helpful police officer laboriously prepared a police report on an elderly typewriter. Back at the passport office, I carefully completed the application for a replacement passport, enclosed two new passport photos, my birth certificate, the old expired Australian passport and the Fijian Police report as my supporting documents.

'We don't issue full replacement passports in these circumstances anymore, but an emergency temporary passport that will last a month will be ready for you in two days.' The lady told me cheerfully and true to her word it was.

It was hard to believe it was all that easy. 'Perhaps the police don't know as much as you fear,' I told myself. 'Surely if they knew that Harry Gordon had been using the Rob passport they would have flagged my name and I would have been arrested. On the other hand, perhaps it is not easy for them to do that in Fiji and they are just waiting for me to arrive back in New Zealand before arresting me?'

I considered again travelling to a different destination. 'No!' I told myself sternly. 'You must return to Kristine no matter what happens, you can't just leave her dangling there, this nonsense has to stop now.' It was now Friday 30 October, some 12 days since we had parted in Raratonga, but now at last in my daily telephone call to her I was able to tell Kristine that I would be returning to her in New Zealand the following day. I telephoned her again just after checking in my bag and receiving my boarding pass the following day, saying: 'I will see you in a few hours darling.'

After going through the departure gate I stopped for the formality of clearance through customs and immigration prior to boarding the aeroplane. The immigration official squinted at his computer screen. 'Mr Gordon, we don't have a record of your arrival in Fiji, when did you say you arrived?' he asked casually.

I told him the same story about arriving two weeks ago by yacht that was associated with a regatta and about losing my passport. Without hesitating he radioed ahead and arranged for my baggage to be offloaded.

'You will need to sort this out with my superior Mr Gordon, I'm sorry we can't let you on this flight but don't worry there is another flight later today, the airline will transfer you.'

Later in the airport immigration office I explained the story again to the duty superior officer and gave him the name of a yacht I had seen and remembered from Raratonga.

'Oh Mr Gordon, this is a serious matter, we know that yacht, it's on our computer records, they have been here before several times but this time they didn't check in with immigration, mmmm, that's quite a serious offence. Now what you need to do Mr Gordon is to telephone or go back to the Island Resort where the yachts in the regatta stayed, they will have records. Please arrange for a statement from the manager of the resort giving details of the yacht's arrival and your check in,' he instructed me in a serious official voice.

'OK, I will try', I told him, 'but I didn't ever check into

the resort, after leaving the yacht. I just caught the normal commuter boat across to the mainland,' I said quickly. 'I don't know if there will be any records.'

'Well you are not going anywhere until we sort this out Mr Gordon. It's a serious offence to bring a vessel into Fiji without customs clearance, how do we know this isn't some drug smuggling operation?' I left the airport and returned on Sunday, the following day, to see him again. 'I have been in contact with the Island Resort and they have no record of me or the yacht!' I told him.

'Well, Mr Gordon, this is a serious matter, my head of department will decide what to do with you on Monday morning when he returns to work. You must come back tomorrow,' he said in his most serious voice.

The following morning his mood seemed completely different when I saw him. 'We are going to allow you to leave on the next flight Mr Gordon. My boss says that it is more trouble to keep you than to let you go,' he said with a chuckle and almost before I knew it I was on the aeroplane. To my great surprise there were no police waiting for me and I wasn't arrested on my arrival at Auckland Airport on 3 October some 25 days after leaving. 'Why aren't the police here? What do they know and what does it all mean?' I wondered as Kristine collected me.

Although she was very pleased to see me, Kristine wanted some answers, she had run a search of me on the internet and now had a much more accurate picture of who I was. I provided her with as little information as I could. I gave her an undertaking that I would return to Australia on 7 November to sort out my legal issues once and for all. In the following days I reviewed my situation and found it far less than satisfactory. I had not worked or produced any income for six weeks except for a small payment from the accident insurance fund. I had funded all the costs of the wedding, the honeymoon and the Fijian excursion from my cash reserve and it was now almost gone. Although I had persuaded Versatile Buildings Ltd to let me return to my selling position it would probably take several weeks before I could generate income. I contacted the real estate agent who had sold me the St Johns house and instructed him to sell it quickly for me. I didn't need a profit from it. I just wanted to unload at market value so that the mortgage and a secured loan could be cleared.

I applied for a proper passport in the name of Harry Gordon with the New Zealand passport office in Auckland to replace the emergency passport that had been issued to me in Fiji and it was in my hands in a couple of weeks. I tried to tidy up my personal and customer commercial files at Versatile Buildings as much as I could but there were loose ends everywhere. I really needed a few months to stabilise my income and sell the St Johns home in order to clear all my creditors and have some order in my personal affairs.

I learned that in my absence after the honeymoon my new bride had discussed my real name and witness protection status story with some of her close friends and family, including her son and son-in-law – both policemen. None of her friends and family had or have any personal loyalty to me and several didn't particularly like me. I believed it was only a matter of time before one of them reported me. I also believed that if I had any hope of controlling the legal process, I had to meet with Sheila and go to a lawyer before the police became involved.

I had to face up to it or run away. There was no more time and no more options. It was time to go.

In planning my return to Sydney I reasoned that although the police may or may not have yet connected the identity of Rob with Harry Gordon, as I hadn't been arrested at Auckland airport on my return from Raratonga there was no reason to suppose I would be arrested as soon as I arrived in Sydney.

My general intention was to make contact with Sheila after I arrived and arrange for us both to go into our family solicitor together. He would have to work out what laws we had broken and how to proceed to resolve it all. There was no doubt that we had both broken some laws. Although Sheila had never been paid anything by AMP, she had made a false life insurance claim and I had acquired then travelled on a false passport.

'Fortunately for us nobody has lost any money and there are no victims so it isn't really a serious matter,' I told myself as I sat on the aeroplane on my way to Sydney. 'It's going to be awfully embarrassing for us. We will both probably be charged and have to appear in court with our names and photos in the newspapers but I doubt that either of us will get a jail sentence because, after all nobody lost any money.'

I concluded that this type of legal case would take months to get started and with a little bit of luck I would be allowed to return to New Zealand to earn some money while the whole thing was being sorted out.

13

Arrested and jailed

NOVEMBER 2005

As soon as I arrived at Sydney airport I was arrested by the NSW police. In that first interview with them I learned that they were aware of the connection between Rob and Harry Gordon as Sheila had made a comprehensive statement to them that was a mixture of truth and half-truth and omissions. It was very clear that they knew very little else except the detail of Sheila's statement. If she hadn't contacted them they would never have known. I declined to make a statement to them until I could take legal advice but confirmed that I had known of the life insurance claim and had travelled on Rob's passport.

'I have returned to Sydney to clear this thing up so as long as you charge me with something that more or less resembles the truth I will plead guilty,' I told the police in the first interview. 'I need bail so that I can consult with my lawyer before making a full statement but rest assured I will be pleading guilty. I have returned for legal closure.'

I asked and was allowed to make two telephone calls from my mobile telephone before my belongings were taken away and I was locked up. I telephoned my brother in New Zealand and asked him to collect my car and some personal papers from my office at Versatile Buildings. I also asked him to collect my remaining personal belongings stored in the basement of my St Johns home and to assist the real estate agent in any way he could with the sale of the home, explaining that the funds were needed to clear my creditors.

I telephoned Kristine and explained that I had been arrested at the airport. I thanked her for her love and commitment to me but released her from all obligations to me given that my future was so uncertain. There was no way of knowing how and when it would all end.

I was held in the police cells overnight and appeared before a magistrate in Waverley Court the following morning with an application for bail. I was shocked to find that the police prosecutor opposed bail and twisted the facts to make it appear as if I had arrived in the country with a number of false passports in my possession and was a flight risk. 'That was so untruthful,' I told the policeman later. 'You know that I had my own real New Zealand passport and an old expired real Australian passport. The only fake one was the Rob passport. You know I returned to Australia for legal closure. I have told you I will make a full statement as soon as I can consult with my lawyer. You could see in my diary that I was planning to see my lawyer. I am going to plead guilty so why did misrepresent my intentions?' I asked, honestly curious. It was obvious that I had a great deal to learn about the prosecution process.

After my initial hearing in court I was locked in a cell for three days with six other prisoners in the basement of the Surry Hills Police Station that I later learned is used as a temporary storage area for remand prisoners until a place can be found for them within the prison system. The cell was approximately 10 metres long by 10 metres wide. Apart from the steel bar door it was all concrete. Three walls each had a concrete ledge about one metre wide that was about half a metre off the floor. There were three thin foam rubber mattresses, each with two blankets, on the ledge of each wall allowing sitting and sleeping space for a total of nine prisoners in the cell.

The wall nearest to the corridor had no ledge and a stainless steel toilet had been placed in the centre of it, facing into the cell in an almost throne like position to maximise the lack of privacy. On the top of the toilet cistern there was a stainless steel sink with cold water for washing and drinking. We all remained in the same clothing and underwear we had been arrested in and there were no arrangements for bathing, showering or exercise.

We were each issued with a 300 millilitre carton of milk and an individual portion of breakfast cereal each morning. In the middle of the day we were each issued with two large greasy sausage rolls for our lunch and in the late afternoon we were each issued with two meat pies and an apple for our dinner.

Each time the guard came to our cell to issue our food he was questioned by the other prisoners about how long we would remain there. 'Fucked if I know and fucked if I care,' he informed them every time. Because the thought of sitting on the throne toilet in front of the other prisoners was abhorrent to me I didn't eat anything for the three days to avoid creating waste within my system. Five of the other prisoners were drug addicts and each of them was going through their own private agony of coping with the lack of drugs. They seemed to sleep for 16 hours a day but when they were awake they were often paranoid, unstable, emotional and dangerous people. It took considerable skill and concentration for me to endure a conversation with each of them without causing offence.

Finally, without warning or explanation, four of us were taken from the cell and loaded onto a prison truck and taken to Silverwater Prison. I noticed a clock in the reception area and noted our arrival time as 11.00pm. We were processed through a system that included fingerprinting and photographs. Our clothing was removed and when naked we were each searched to ensure that we didn't have any drugs on us before we were issued with prison clothing. The clothing consisted of two pairs of green shorts and T-shirts, one green jumper, two pairs of green socks and a cheap pair of white gym shoes. They had run out of underwear during my induction so I was not issued with any underpants and in fact didn't have access to underpants for another two months.

Some time after midnight I was issued with two sheets, two blankets and let into a small two-person cell where an unknown prisoner was asleep on the bottom bunk. Although he was asleep his small television was blaring on a steel shelf. With my previous experience of paranoid, unstable personalities at Surry Hills, I was more than a little nervous about disturbing him so I just crawled onto the top bunk and snuggled into my blankets without unpacking or making the bed up properly. In the morning I found that he was a nice middle-aged chap with a drinking problem who was in prison for drink-related offences.

I was taken from the cell at 10.00am and escorted to an arrival interview with a prison physiologist, who asked me standard questions about if I was depressed and had any thoughts about harming myself or suicide. I indicated that although I was unhappy to be in prison I did not believe myself to be clinically depressed. I was to learn that the formal prison system for managing any prisoners with clinical depression was to take away all their clothing except their underpants then lock them in a bare cell where the light was on 24 hours a day with just a foam mattress and two blankets for four days. They would then be taken back to the psychologist and asked 'How are you feeling now?' Most, of course, declared at that point that they were cured of their clinical depression and asked to be allowed back to a normal cell with their clothing, and standard privileges. This system taught all prisoners that anyone foolish enough to share their real emotional thoughts or fears with a prison psychologist would be punished.

The same rule applied to almost all interaction with prison authority. Any question we were ever asked by a prison official had an existing standard answer that was acceptable to them. There was no reward for truthfulness and often a significant punishment so it was discarded. The psychologist was able to give me some basic information on prison privileges. I learned that until I was allocated a prison job that paid about $16 per week I would be credited with about $13 to my prison bank account each week as a sort of prison tobacco allowance payment. The following week I would be able to use that money to buy tobacco and or many other items including paper, envelopes and stamps to write and send letters with.

Although I was pleased to learn that the government was going to give me $13 each week in case I needed to smoke tobacco, I did the mental arithmetic of $13 times 8,500 prisoners equals $110,500 times 52 weeks equals $5,746,000 per year. Wow! More than $5.5 million of taxpayers money is spent each year so that prisoners can smoke. 'Perhaps they are trying to kill us with lung cancer,' I mused.

Notwithstanding my misgivings as a taxpayer about this waste I desperately wanted to write to people as soon as I could so it was very good news for me. Upon my return from the psychologist I was issued with a salad roll and peanut butter sandwich for my lunch. This was the first food I had eaten since my arrest, four days earlier and I was famished. A little later our wing of about 100 prisoners were all taken to a concrete yard for two hours' exercise before we were all issued with a corned beef salad dinner in a small aluminium foil dish, rather like a budget third-world airline meal, for our dinner, as we were locked away in our cells at 3.00pm for the night.

There was a toilet and shower in the corner of our cell next to the door so I was able to sit on the toilet with the shower curtain and noise of the television providing a reasonable level of privacy from my cell mate. It wasn't dignified but it was reasonable under the circumstances. The next day was spent in the cell except for two sessions of two hours in the exercise yard again. I saw my first real prison violence. A prisoner who I learned later was incorrectly identified as a child molester, was savagely beaten and kicked in the yard by another prisoner. The guards did not rush in to stop the violence but in due course wandered into the yard and took both of them away and I never saw them again.

The few days that followed were all the same until unexpectedly on Sunday after lunch I was taken to the reception area and given my crumpled street clothes to put on again and then placed in a holding cell with several other men before being loaded onto a truck and driven to Newcastle Central Court where I was locked in the police cells overnight that were similar to the Surry Hills police cells. The following morning without the benefit of a shave or a wash I was taken to Raymond Terrace Court House and locked in the cells below the court.

The duty legal aid solicitor, visited me in the interview booth next to my cell and asked if I wanted him to represent me.

I told him that I didn't have any money and didn't think that I qualified for legal aid and since I was intending to plead guilty anyway there wasn't any point. He offered to enter the guilty plea on my behalf free of charge. 'I am here anyway Harry!' but more importantly he also agreed to act on my behalf for a delayed fee in a minor way in some of my private and family law matters.

'I never expected to be held in prison on remand, it is most important that my home in New Zealand is sold and all my creditors paid. I could sure use a little help with that but I have no idea when I can pay you.'

'I am happy to help Harry' he replied warmly. When I did go up to court the prosecutor asked for the matter was stood over until 22 December to allow them more time and bail was formally refused on the basis of the same nonsense that I had several false passports, no community ties and was a flight risk. After another night in the cells at Newcastle I was delivered back to Silverwater Prison on Tuesday 15 November and learned that every Tuesday is a lockdown day at Silverwater with all prisoners remaining in their cells without exercise all day long.

Prisoners at Silverwater were then allowed, I think, three, one-hour visits each week and the following day I was told I had a visitor and taken to the visitors centre. On the walk there I tried to think who it may be. Perhaps one of my siblings or a close former business associate had come or perhaps Kristine had flown over to offer her love and support as my wife. I was grouped with other prisoners with visitors and we were all ordered to change into white overalls that had zips up the back. It must have been a security measure to limit drug smuggling into the prison.

When at last I was cleared into the visiting area I was

surprised to find David and Caroline Collon waiting to visit me. They owned and operated an earthmoving business that I had done business with for many years before my disappearance and although we had enjoyed a friendly working relationship with each other, we had not been personal friends so I was surprised by their visit. They were so warm and friendly I almost cried.

'You don't need to explain anything to us, we don't need reasons, we haven't come to judge you Harry, we have come as your friends to support you, how can we help?' said David kindly. They had never been to a prison before and like me found the whole thing more than a little daunting but they had come. Their visit was a wonderful act of kindness to me and I will always be grateful. During the visit David mentioned that he had leukaemia but he was in remission and was so confident about his prognosis that he had just started up a new business that complemented his earthmoving company.

'I will be happy to give you a job when you get out of prison, we are your friends,' he told me cheerfully. After their visit they corresponded with me regularly and they visited me some months later when I was in Muswellbrook prison but tragically David's leukaemia returned. He was very sick when I last saw him and he died before I was released from prison. The phrase, 'A friend in need is a friend indeed' comes to mind when I think of him and I think of him often.

Two days later I had another visitor and once again on the walk there I hoped it may be one of my siblings or Kristine but it turned out to be Simon, a childhood friend of my daughter Josaphine. Out of all the people in the world that I had relationships with he too had taken the time and trouble to visit me. 'How strange life and relationships are' I reflected as I walked back to my cell.

On Saturday 19 November I received my first buy-up

package of paper, stamps and envelopes that allowed me to communicate with the outside world for the first time in the 12 days I had been in prison. That night I wrote a 10 point, 14-page letter to my duty solicitor detailing my current assets and liabilities along with my plan to pay my creditors once the New Zealand house was sold. I included a draft letter to each of my creditors and asked him to write to them indicating my intentions and plan. I asked him also to write to the New Zealand real estate agent indicating that he acted for me so that any further signatures required to complete a sale could be expedited quickly. Finally I asked him to place a caveat or some other legal restraint on Sheila to prevent the sale of our Australian real estate and to write to her solicitors seeking a no-fuss 50/50 settlement. I also wrote to my brother giving him details of the New Zealand real estate agent and asking him to render any assistance to the agent or solicitor in order to facilitate a quick sale of the property. Finally I wrote to Kristine asking her forgiveness for the great wrong I had done her and again releasing her from any obligation to me.

The following day I was taken into a classification meeting with several prison officials who neither identified themselves nor gave any details of how or why they arrived at their assessment of me but after the meeting I was moved to a different wing and into a new cell with a new cell mate. My routine of mostly being locked in the cell with two sessions of exercise continued over the next few days with meals in the budget airline type foil trays. On Thursday 24 November I was advised that I had been allocated a job in the laundry and was taken off to work to fold sheets and towels for six hours each day.

My days drifted on until Wednesday 30 November when I was moved to a new job as the clerk in a small textile factory within the prison compound. The unit had about 20 sewing machines, a cutting table and normal sorting and storage areas. It seemed to be mostly staffed by Asian inmates. The supervision and systems of work were like visiting a 1950s factory in a time warp. The prison officers were so busy with their social interaction that they rarely visited the factory floor where there was a wonderful holiday atmosphere.

My job, mostly computer work, involved creating production schedules, cutting sheets, payroll, invoicing, etc. I also had to maintain the quality control and occupational health and safety records. The prisoner who trained me explained that we didn't really complete the quality checks nor did we give our inmate employees, many of whom who didn't speak English, any safety induction training. It was a fraud!

'Fill out all the forms in your own handwriting,' he explained 'but you need to change the signatures so they don't all look the same.'

For some reason, perhaps years of conditioning, I was filled with shock and horror to the extent that I quickly reported the situation to the prison officer in charge. 'The safety training in particular is our most basic duty of care!' I thundered. 'This can't be allowed to continue.' His bright blue eyes looked out at me over his half round spectacles with genuine surprise. 'Oh fuck, you're not going to be one of those are you?' he asked, and in a heartbeat I remembered where I was.

'Absolutely not!' I replied and in no time at all I was falsifying records and forging signatures as if I had been doing it all my life.

At the end of each day we returned to our accommodation wings for an hour or so of social interaction before being issued with our dinner in the foil tray and were locked into our cells for the night.

Much of the social interaction in the hour or so before we

were locked away involved the buying and selling of drugs. The place was awash with drugs of every kind – heroin, speed, marijuana and all manner of tablets. Several of the people in my wing were supposedly spending more than $2,000 a week from their outside resources to support their drug requirements.

On Saturday 10 December I had a brief visit from the duty solicitor, at the Silverwater legal visits room. He explained that he was down in Sydney on family business and it was no trouble for him to call in. He indicated that he hadn't yet received the letter I had written him but would act on it when it came to hand.

He had also prepared and presented me with a formal quotation of $5,000 if I wanted him to represent me in the criminal matter. I indicated I would think about it but in the meantime my primary concern was not the criminal matter but for him to assist the process of selling my New Zealand home and arranging an orderly settlement of my creditors. Before leaving the solicitor also informed me that he had news that my daughter Josaphine was now back in Australia.

He understood that the police had arrested and charged her with something but she was out on bail. I didn't know what to make of that news.

14

Cessnock Prison

DECEMBER 2005

O n Sunday 11 December without any explanation or
warning, I was given 15 minutes' notice that I was to
be moved to Cessnock Jail. Of course I didn't need to pack a
bag as all my prison issue belongings except the clothes I was
standing in were left behind so I didn't need much notice. Six
other inmates and I were all searched, then handcuffed before
being loaded into a small compartment in the prison truck. As
soon as the door was closed, before the engine even started
my fellow inmates removed hidden cigarettes from their shoes
and clothing. One of the prisoners pulled down his pants
and removed some drugs he had hidden in a plastic bag up
his bottom. By the time we reached Cessnock prison, some six
hours later, the air was so thick with tobacco and marijuana
smoke that I could hardly breath but the prison officers who let
us out didn't seem to notice or care when they opened the door
to let us out.

The induction process was similar to Silverwater Prison where after lengthy delays we were all individually fingerprinted and photographed, although there was no new issue of clothing. What we stood in on arrival was all that we were allowed. When I asked, perhaps too forcefully, about additional clothing and underpants I was subjected to my first violence by a prison officer. It wasn't serious, just half a dozen mild punches really, but it was enough to put me in my place.

I shared my first few days in Cessnock Prison with an elderly, short little man who had leathery skin and the look of a retired jockey. His bushy grey eyebrows undulated gently as he spoke but sadly his mouth didn't seem to move at all. It was as if the words were coming indistinctly out of the key hole in a door so I really only understood about every fourth word. I participated in conversation with him as best I could with nods and murmurs but on the third night tears started to roll down his unfortunate leathery cheeks at what must have been an important emotional moment in his monologue. Clearly a fulsome and relevant response was required from me at this point. 'Damn all women!' I ventured. He smiled at me and wiped away the tears, satisfied it seems with my response and empathy. Even in prison social skills are vital!

The remand wing where I was housed at Cessnock Prison was a three-story building constructed around an enclosed central courtyard that was used for exercise when we were let out. It had a very fluid population of about one 130 prisoners who were constantly arriving from their initial court hearing then leaving to a different wing or prison after they were sentenced. The top floor of about 40 prisoners was allocated to prisoners who needed to be segregated from the main prison population for their own protection and they were separated from us by locked steel gates on the stairwell.

The bottom floor was mostly setup as two men cells for new arrivals on three arms with the guard's offices on the fourth arm. The middle floor had about 30 single man cells on three arms and a central shower block on the fourth arm as the only ablution facilities in the cells were toilets and a cold water basin.

About a week or so after my arrival I was moved into a one man cell by myself on the middle floor. It was my first private space in six weeks and more importantly the first time in six weeks I had sat on a toilet in a room by myself. Early on in my time at Cessnock one of the illiterate inmates asked me to read him a recently delivered legal aid solicitor's letter to him and accepted my offer to write a reply on his behalf. From him the news quickly spread that I was a gifted letter writer and in the following three months at Cessnock Prison I wrote 63 letters on behalf of other inmates. Although the demand dropped off when I was moved to another prison in March, within a year I had written more than 150 letters for other prisoners. Some of the letters were to legal aid solicitors, some to parole boards, some to magistrates for consideration during sentencing and some were to family, wives and sweethearts.

Because I had always assumed that an important element of justice was that it be delivered quickly and fairly, I was shocked to meet some people had already been in remand for more than two years and still didn't know when they may have their day in court. It became clear to me that anyone on remand on a first offence was far more likely to plead and/or be found guilty than someone who was out on bail. Although it is technically possible for accused people on remand to meet with a lawyer to discuss the case, the reality is that most of their energy is expended just fighting to survive in their violent new prison environment.

My personal correspondence at this time was also

considerable as I wrote to Kristine almost every day, to my siblings on a regular basis and replied to letters and cards from various other former friends who wrote to me.

My routine was now quite different from Silverwater Prison as nobody in the remand wing at Cessnock has any paid employment. In the mornings we were let out of our cells for about two hours between the hours of 9.30am and 11.30am before being issued with lunch and locked back in our cells. We were let out again in the afternoons for two or more hours between 1.00pm to 3.00pm before being issued with our dinner and locked away in our cells at about 3.30pm for the night. We spent a total of 19 hours or more each day locked away in the cells. As soon as we were let go each morning I would make my way down to the central courtyard and run 40 laps, about 3.5 kilometres, around it before shaving and showering in the central shower block. In the afternoon I would find visitors at my door, some collecting letters I had written for them the night before, some wanting new letters written or discussed and some just wanting to talk. It was a very busy time and I often wished I could just leave my door closed to escape the constant flow.

Early on Thursday 22 December I was taken to reception and issued with my street clothes to wear to court again. My $3,000 suit and now very dirty dress shirt had been crumpled up in a ball with my shoes in a standard prison storage sack. There was no arrangement for hanging clothes; they were all just stuffed into sacks.

In due course I arrived in court only to have it stood over again until 13 February to allow the prosecution more time to prepare their case. 'What do they need to prepare?' I asked the solicitor who was in court again. 'I am pleading guilty, why do they need more time for goodness sake?' But he had no explanation. He also informed me that he had not as yet undertaken most of the tasks I had asked him to complete relating to my creditors and the family law matter. 'Don't you want to do the work?' I asked him.

'To tell you the truth I hate family law. I am a criminal law specialist but I will find someone else who can handle it for you,' he replied cheerfully. I returned to the prison that night deeply dissatisfied with the solicitor and the outcome of the day.

On Christmas day, some 49 days after my arrest I was told my daughter Josaphine had come to visit and I was allowed a one hour visit with her. The arrangements and white overalls with the zip up the back were almost the same as Silverwater Prison. Although my situation and hers were very grave it was wonderful to see her again. 'I came as soon as I could Daddy. I'm afraid I just had to abandon most of my belongings in Brunei but I needed to get here as soon as I could and whatever happens I will support you every step of the way. I only knew what I had read in the newspapers so I went to the police as soon as I arrived to find out where and how you were. They arrested then charged me with conspiracy. They opposed bail and said in court that I was a flight risk but it was too ridiculous for the magistrate to believe as I had just flown in from Brunei and gone to the police station of my own free will so I am out on bail.

'I suspect you have told me few fibs in the past few years that may get me into trouble,' she said. 'You probably weren't in a real witness protection program and other stuff that you told me was probably wrong but I don't care, you are my family and you can count me no matter what!' she declared unconditionally. The one hour visit wasn't nearly enough for us to get through the business we had together.

The most important matter for discussion was what arrangements to make for Chriseb's care if she was convicted of some offence and sent to prison at the same time as me. My initial response was that she wasn't guilty of anything but in the unlikely event that she was convicted and imprisoned my brother or sister should be asked to care for Chriseb.

'Daddy you haven't read the police brief. I have! They are the reason you are here. They gave you up to Sheila. It's all in the official transcript. They arranged for Mum to fly to New Zealand so they could have a meeting with her about you. It's all on record. On their advice Mum went to the police and made her statement.'

We spent some time discussing the possibility that she would be convicted. 'Don't be in any doubt that I am in deep shit Daddy. The fact that I am not guilty and the police know I am not guilty won't stop them from persisting with this,' she said bitterly.

In the end we decided that although we had to plan for the worst, with a little bit of luck, if my sentence was about six months long including time served she may be able to delay her court case for one reason or another until after my prison term had ended so if the worst happened I would be there to care for Chriseb if she was incarcerated.

'We will just have to hold our breath on this one,' I told her before moving on to the subject of where she was going to live. Since her arrival back in Australia she had been living in Brisbane with her old boyfriend who had moved home from New Zealand after he left our St Johns home. She was now ready to arrange a change in her bail conditions and move into our home at North Arm Cove that was just half an hour away from the Raymond Terrace court house, allowing her to make cost effective appearances in court. It was also only an hour and a bit from Cessnock Prison so she would be able to visit me on a regular basis.

All too soon the one-hour visit was ending and we agreed she would come again on 7 January when she had moved herself down from Brisbane. Finally, in the remaining minutes we discussed my legal situation and I asked her to find a local solicitor who handled family law matters to take over from him.

'I don't need anybody in court with me for the criminal matter but I do need the New Zealand home sold, creditors paid and a caveat on our NSW properties to prevent your mother from selling them on us and hiding the money,' I told her.

'I will look after it,' were her parting words as she was hurried out by the guard. Not long after she left I was given the gift package of underpants and handkerchiefs she had left for me and that afternoon I wore underpants again for the first time in more than 45 days.

After Josaphine's visit I reflected on the actions of my siblings and my relationship with them. 'Perhaps Josaphine hasn't quite got it right,' I pondered and continued to write letters to them but became much more cautious about what I wrote to them and the relationships in general.

I also had many other people to exchange letters with including Kristine, who had indicated that she may be willing to forgive me and allow me a second chance depending on the length of my sentence and the quality of my repentance.

The days drifted by until Josaphine visited me again on 7 January and this time she brought Chriseb with her allowing wonderful grandpa/grandson time together. She also informed me that she had found and engaged another solicitor, to replace the duty solicitor and he would call on me at the prison in a week or so.

I quickly wrote out a note for her to take to the solicitor formally requesting that he release my file to the new solicitor. Josaphine also informed me that she had found a barrister who was willing to represent me in court for my guilty plea. 'He is not expensive Daddy and after all he knows the law and can argue for the lightest possible sentence on your behalf,' she told me before giving me his details.

I had taken a large envelope of various papers to and from that visit, and every subsequent visit, with Josaphine offering the honest and simple explanation to the guards that they were legal papers. One of the more curious aspects of prison procedure was that after every visit I, and all the other prisoners, had to strip naked and be thoroughly searched before returning to our cells to ensure we were not smuggling drugs but the guards never checked my paperwork envelope. I could have smuggled half a kilo of drugs in every time. 'There is no logic, just process,' I mused as I walked back each time.

After Josaphine left I made arrangements to have the North Arm Cove telephone number formally listed as a number I was able to call from the prison phone. There was always a queue to use the phone and it cost about $2.30 to call her for three minutes but it made a real difference to her life and mine. After the arrangement was made I called her at least four times each week just for a quick 'I'm okay are you OK?' type of call.

In the week following her visit I was subjected to a violent attack. A group of inmates had accosted me for tobacco the previous week and when I explained that I didn't smoke they instructed me to order some tobacco for them in my next buy up due to arrive on Wednesday. On Thursday morning when I took my daily shower after running my laps, a group of them came into the shower block and asked me where their tobacco was. I told them that I hadn't ordered any for them as I didn't have much money in my prison account and the little money I did have was needed for stationery, and stamps for the letters I wrote. I managed to stay on my feet during the beating and protected my face from the worst blows with my arms but I was badly shaken as well as physically damaged by the experience.

I resolved to always shower in my underpants from that day onwards as although there had not been anything sexual about the beating my nakedness had increased my sense of vulnerability and had somehow increased the indignity of the experience. Although the beating was common knowledge, I was never questioned about it by the guards. I recovered quickly and was relieved that in the following few days, several of the most aggressive members of the group left the remand wing and the remaining group didn't feel strong enough to act as a gang again. Violence remained a constant fact of life in the wing, at least twice a week someone was beaten or knifed during some sort of dispute, mostly over drugs or payment for drugs but I managed to avoid it for the remainder of my time in Cessnock.

The following week on Thursday 19 January, as arranged, the new solicitor that Josaphine had found for me came to visit me and we had a very productive meeting about the domestic and family law matters I needed him to handle for me. I had prepared copious notes for him and at the end of the meeting I was more than satisfied that he knew what was required of him.

At the time of my arrest I weighed a healthy if slightly chubby 84 kilos. Since my arrival at Cessnock Prison I had the opportunity to weigh myself every day on a set of scales just inside the door of the first-aid area where the nurse issued medication each day. I had arrived at Cessnock weighing 80 kilos, my ideal weight, but in the month I had been in Cessnock my weight dropped to 74 kilos.

On Friday 20 January I started to suffer from stomach pain after dinner and at first thought that something I had eaten didn't agree with me but after going to the toilet and having a vomit the pain just seemed to get worse. By 10.00pm I couldn't stand the pain any more and pressed the emergency buzzer. A plump officer with sad watery eyes and a long grey beard, like Santa gone to seed, came to look at me, then the prison nurse, who for some reason called me 'lovey'. In due course an ambulance was called and I was taken to hospital.

Friday night passed in a blur of pain and drug-induced sleep but on Saturday morning I awoke with only mild pain and felt much better. I found myself in an open ward of Cessnock Public Hospital with two prison officers guarding me. The female officer seemed fast asleep. The male officer on the other hand was bright and alert. As he chatted with me he first ate two egg sandwiches that his wife had prepared for his breakfast, and then as I was 'nil by mouth' he ate my hospital breakfast. I noticed that his feet didn't touch the floor as he swung his fat little legs to and fro under the chair with contentment.

In due course I was taken to another room where a pleasant young woman completed an ultrasound examination of my stomach and announced that I had gallstones, she could see them clearly in the ultrasound. 'Fancy that,' I thought 'I know nothing about them.'

I was taken back to the ward to wait for the doctor. He was shaking with rage when he did arrive. With wild eyes and trembling hands he stammered that my daughter had somehow discovered his mobile telephone number and had telephoned him 10 times in the past two hours trying to find out my condition. His whole body was quivering with indignation. 'If she calls one more time I will report her to the police!' he threatened 'How dare she?'

'My daughter is my next of kin and will be worried about me,' I suggested to him. 'As, in this instance, you are my treatment doctor, she will be telephoning you to ensure that I am all right, it all sounds very normal to me,' I concluded in my most reasonable voice.

'I don't have to tell her anything!' he shouted.

Much later that night in my hospital bed, with a different shift of guards on duty I wanted to go to the toilet. Both guards had their eyes closed, one was gently snoring and the other was passing wind with a pop, pop, pop sound like a small one cylinder marine engine starting up. I pretended to snore very loudly until I heard one of them stir, then I made a huge theatrical production of waking up before asking to be taken to the toilet.

On Sunday afternoon a nurse came and informed the guards, on a different shift, that I was to be released shortly and she had a brief conversation with them about my prognosis and treatment options. I felt as if I was being treated like a horse at the vet and sought to involve myself. 'Excuse me,' I interrupted, 'I need to participate in my own medical treatment so you need to discuss these matters with me, not them; I am the sick person here!'

'Wot you need lad is a bit of newmility and prison is going to teach you that!' said one of the officers.

'Oh quite right,' I replied in rapid retreat. 'And some of us have much to be numble about.'

I was returned to prison on Sunday night and didn't learn that my gallstones were connected to rapid weight loss until Kristine sent me an internet printout about it. It was also from her rather than the medical staff that I learned that by limiting fat and dairy food intake I could prevent future gallstone attacks.

15

The law and Kristine

FEBRUARY 2006

The days and the weeks drifted on, with Josaphine and Chriseb's visits each Saturday and letters from my many friends being my only connection with the outside world. Josaphine and I had a very important breakthrough offer in a letter from Peter and Helen Martin, friends from my former life, at this time. In a normal exchange of letters I had shared my fears with them about what would happen to Chriseb if Josaphine had to go to prison at the same time as me. Helen wrote back immediately and offered herself as his carer and their home as his home in that eventuality for as long as we needed them. This was a huge relief to us and we will owe them a debt of gratitude for that offer for the rest of our lives.

Chriseb's care had been a nightmare for us until their offer. Josaphine and I both cried with relief during one of her visits to me as we shared the news.

On the domestic legal front we had some bad news. 'The

186

real estate agent has had several buyers and your brother has been dealing with him but for some reason they can't seem to get the legal act together to finalise a deal,' Josaphine told me before we agreed that the solicitor would need to take more energetic interest in the process. 'We want to sell it at a slightly discounted price, people want to buy it, gosh how hard can it be?' I asked rhetorically.

On 8 February a barrister that Josaphine had found for me came to visit me in prison. In my conversation with him I tried to impress upon him my belief that the most important element in my forthcoming hearing was the need to refute Sheila's allegation that Josaphine had been involved.

By arrangement with the prison Josaphine collected my suit from prison storage on a Saturday visit and returned it on Saturday 11 February with a clean white shirt for my appearance on Monday.

'There is no doubt that I will have to appear on my own behalf,' I said. 'It will be the only chance I will ever have in open court to refute your mother's lies. There will be no hearing on Monday. The barrister has told me that. All that happens on Monday is that the magistrate will set time aside in the coming week for a full hearing. Let's not inform the prosecutor of our intentions too quickly by giving the barrister the flick too soon,' I replied and as we were talking I wrote a termination of services letter to the barrister for her to take away and give to him a couple of days before the hearing.

As we expected on Monday the magistrate set aside time on 23 February and Josaphine delivered the termination letter to the barrister on Tuesday 21 February. I was delighted when the police visited me in the cells below the court on the 23 February to ask where my barrister was. I have no idea if I did a good job or bad job in representing myself on the day. The magistrate asked for the prosecutor's final advice before sentencing me.

I was sentenced to 18 months in prison with an earliest release in 15 months. It was much worse than I had hoped for but not as bad as I had feared in my worst nightmares. On the next Saturday visit Josaphine informed me that she had already made an application for an appeal and was attempting to get the legal-aid barrister to represent me. 'We will need another barrister to represent you at the appeal. Appeals are all about points of law, it's not something you can do yourself.'

'I don't think I qualify for legal aid,' I told her.

'Right at this point, until ownership of the NSW properties is resolved you technically do qualify. Don't worry I will fix it up, you don't deserve that sentence, it's too silly. You are being punished for protecting me,' she said.

On 9 March, as a formally sentenced criminal, I was moved out of the remand wing into wing two of the prison a block of similar size to the remand wing but its yard was opened to the rest of the prison each day allowing access to all the prison grounds and had available interaction with about 300 prisoners in total every day. Most of the prisoners were allocated prison jobs so I quickly applied and was approved to join the ground maintenance crew, mostly on gardening and lawn mowing duties. It was a welcome relief to stand on grass after months of concrete. As a medium security prison the prisoners here were no more violent than those I had been with in the remand wing but because we were only locked in our cells for about 12 hours a day, from 7.00pm until 7.00am there was a greater level of violence just because more time was available and larger numbers of prisoners were involved.

I tried to interact with very few people and keep a low profile in order to minimise my risk. Josaphine and Chriseb continued to visit me every Saturday or Sunday and the visits section in this part of the prison was a vast improvement on the remand section. Visits were allowed from 9.00am until 3.00pm in a park garden type setting and visitors could buy us and themselves drinks and food to cook on the barbecues within the visits section. For Chriseb's birthday, Josaphine even arranged for the prison shop to provide a birthday cake so that we could celebrate the day together as a family.

Josaphine was back in court on 13 February, expecting to have a trial date set and when we spoke on the telephone later in the afternoon she gave me the news. 'All the charges against me have been dropped Daddy. The prosecution came into court and said that there wasn't enough evidence against me and they were withdrawing all charges. They did say that they reserve the right to bring other charges against me at some future date.'

It was wonderful news, the best news we could have received. The following Saturday when Josaphine and Chriseb came to visit we almost danced for joy together. Josaphine also briefed me on the meetings she had been having with the legal aid barrister who was to represent me at the appeal the following week. My 18 month sentence consisted of 12 months for conspiracy but three months of that was allowed as a parole period making it really only nine months in prison. Then I had to serve six months for the offence of holding a false passport, making the total time in prison 15 months.

The legal-aid barrister thought it was pointless appealing against the severity of either sentence as too much could go wrong but since both offences were connected there was a good case with lots of precedent for both sentences to be served concurrently. The barrister was confident that she could persuade the court to combine the sentences and reduce my time served to nine months.

When I did arrive at court on 24 March a male barrister had replaced the female barrister who was supposed to represent me. She was apparently needed in another court that day. As my legal-aid representative, this barrister seemed unprepared. But we went into court, he made the application to combine the sentences, the prosecution did not oppose it and unsurprisingly the judge reduced my time to serve by three months, I was to be released in 32 weeks time on 5 November. 'I don't know how much legal aid barristers are paid,' I told Josaphine on the telephone the following day, 'but let's hope it isn't too much.' In truth, despite the result being what we had hoped for it was still a three-month reduction and better than no reduction at all.

In our correspondence we had arranged for Kristine to fly over from New Zealand and visit with me on the weekend of 25 and 26 March. The purpose of the visit was for her to interview me then decide if I was worth waiting for and given a second chance. Josaphine was more than a little cynical about the relationship. 'I know you love her Daddy and whatever you do is okay with me but I am worried that she may be a fairweather wife. When you were in your darkest hour here in prison did she fly over to support you? Did she even ask if you needed anything? When you needed a lawyer did she offer you any financial assistance? When you were worried I may go to prison and there would be nobody to look after Chriseb did she offer to help? Don't give her any power in your financial affairs. Just like Mum, when push comes to shove she will sell you down the river.' It was a heartfelt and appraisal and I was grateful she felt able to offer it to me so honestly and openly.

'You, Chriseb and I love each other unconditionally because we are a not just family we are a highly tribal family with profound loyalty to each other. I can't expect Kristine to be like us, to feel like us nor to have the same sense of family loyalty.

If there is one thing I have learned from your mother it is that I need to lower my expectations in a marriage. It will be the same for you in any romantic relationship you develop kiddo but that is no reason for us to go throughout life without love. It's only a heartbeat in time before we are both dead so we have to accept life the way it comes to us. To use Jack Nicholson's line, this is as good as it gets.'

Kristine did arrive at last, some 20 weeks after my arrest, and the time we spent together during her visit was wonderful. I needed and was able to openly admit and accept responsibility for my dishonesty in describing my past to her and apologise for involving her in a bigamous marriage. In due course she indicated she would consider giving me another chance. We kissed and held each other with as much enthusiasm as the unwritten prison rules allowed and reconnected with one another. It was clear that I was less than the man she had hoped for but still worth the effort. She didn't love me with the intense unconditional loyalty that I may have wished for but she was wonderful and I loved her deeply and sincerely.

Apart from the emotional connection we also discussed matters of a practical nature. Prior to her visit I had explained in my correspondence the difficulty I was having selling the New Zealand home. The tenant had left so the property had no income to cover the monthly mortgage payments, the real estate agent seemed to be in a muddle and my brother, who is very experienced in real estate issues, with multiple tenanted properties of his own seemed to be unable or unwilling to expedite the matter.

Armed with this information Kristine arrived with a document for me to sign allowing her power or attorney in the matter and offered to take responsibility for it. I accepted her offer gratefully and was rewarded by her diligence and skill in preparing the property for sale on her return to New Zealand and securing a buyer within six weeks at almost the same price I had been asking all along.

Unfortunately the six-month delay in selling the house, much of it without rent from a tenant, had created significant costs and default charges, eating up most of the equity so that when my mortgage with the bank and secondary lender were discharged there was only $2,500 left and Kristine needed that to cover her lawyer's costs in providing advice to her when she was being interviewed by the police after my arrest. I had no money left to cover the $8,000 in minor unsecured creditors.

All too soon the visit with Kristine was over and after she had left I tried to make sense of all that she had said and think about how our life together would work after my release. It wasn't at all clear.

16

Muswellbrook Prison

MARCH 2006

On 30 March I was loaded into a compartment on a truck with other prisoners and driven to the low security prison farm at Muswellbrook. At first its low security and farm status seemed incongruous as I was still within a high-security wire compound just the same as any other prison and I learned that out of the prison population of 260 only about 15 prisoners worked on the farm.

The accommodation arrangements were very different from my previous prison experiences as we were housed in groups of 12 in rough hostel type units. Each unit had about eight single-man bedrooms and two double bedrooms housing 12 men in total. There were two bathrooms each with two toilets, two showers and a trough type wash basin. There was a common room with a sink bench, hot plate type stove, refrigerator, television and three tables with fixed bench seating that combined as a kitchen and dining room. We were locked away in our units from 6.00pm at night until 7.00am in the morning but were free to move about within the common areas of the unit at any time of the day or night. After months of living by myself in a single cell almost all my privacy and personal space was gone again.

I was now living in very close quarters with 11 other men, many of whom were dangerous and unstable. I learned that at any given time at least 30 of the prisoners were on reduced privileges of some kind due to testing positive to drugs in a random urine test and they were only the ones who were caught. Some inmates were talkative, some were reclusive, some were morose, and some were paranoid. I hated it.

With my previous prison experience this new environment of even closer proximity to my fellow inmates allowed me to learn even more about them as a group and the effect that prison generally had on them.

If the fear of prison was supposed to be a general deterrent that would prevent people from offending it had clearly failed. No prisoner I ever met had ever been deterred from committing any crime by fear of a potential prison sentence. All were deterred only by their ethical boundaries, opportunity, skills and/or their perception of the risk that they may be caught.

A second function of prison is to change the offender in some way so that he is less likely to reoffend. By adopting the name 'Corrective Services' the prison service has clearly embraced this function as its primary goal but in fact prison has exactly the reverse effect on its inmates. There are many prisoners who have committed a single crime in a lapse of judgment that they regret and they were never going to reoffend and still never will so prison has no effect on their future behaviour.

Most of the prisoners I met were shifted even deeper into their life of crime by prison. The system degrades and humiliates them to believe that they will never fit into normal society. Not only are they more likely to reoffend but their new crimes will probably be more serious and more violent than their original crime. For most inmates, prison is like throwing petrol on a fire. Every day I met people angry, bitter men who really didn't care about anything or anyone who were shortly to be released back into their criminal lives, they were disasters waiting to happen. It didn't make any sense to me.

Within a week I was allocated a job as the clerk in a small vegetable processing factory within the prison compound that employed about 35 prisoners and two supervising guards. My job included prisoner payroll, processing orders into production schedules, preparing dispatch documentation and invoicing plus basic profit and loss accounting work. It was an easy job and highly paid by prison standards. I was earning $65 per week when many of the prisoners working hard in the factory were earning little more than $20 per week. Despite its negligible wage bill and lack of overheads the factory struggled to make a profit. The general relationship between prison officers and prisoners is normally one of benign neglect with random acts of cruelty but because I had a neutral work-related interaction with my supervising guards I quickly developed a functional if somewhat awkward working relationship with them. I really struggled in my relationships with the prisoners. Many of them were constantly asking me to falsify their timesheets and/or give them unauthorised pay increases. 'I can't do that,' I would tell them. 'It would be fraud and I will get into trouble.'

'What can they do to you, you are already in prison, are one of us or one of them?' I was often asked this by angry prisoners but I held firm and followed the rules mostly as a matter of personal ethics and conditioning rather that fear of being caught. The truth was that my work, including the payroll was rarely checked as the supervising guards spent large portions of their days on the telephone or with each other arranging their personal domestic and private commercial lives. Apart from being bone idle and lazy most prison officers were operating some sort of personal scam.

As I settled into my new life I noticed with pleasure that my personal interaction with the outside world blossomed. Josaphine and Chriseb visited me every Saturday and many friends from my former life came to visit me on Sundays. Muswellbrook is in a remote location so apart from the cost of visiting me my friends really had to give up an entire day for each visit so I really was grateful. All of my visitors, including Josaphine, bought food from the prison kiosk in the visitors centre and we ate huge if not elaborate meals together and I started to put on weight again.

During the time I was in prison 48 different people visited me, mostly as couples, many several times and I exchanged letters with more than 90 different friends who offered their support. Because I was now earning more money and the rules permitted me to make overseas phone calls I arranged to have Kristine's telephone number added to my official phone list. Because I telephoned both her and Josaphine every day most of my prison income was spent on telephone calls, stamps and stationery.

Perhaps because of my prison job as a clerk or perhaps some personal characteristic, in contrast to my easy prison employment and pleasant interaction with the outside world, my relationship with some of the other inmates became a dangerous nightmare.

Apart from the normal verbal conflict with them over pay when I was at work I found myself subjected to a very silly physical attack that was more dangerous than it first seemed.

As I was walking around the exercise pathway after work one afternoon I was struck in the head with an egg that had been thrown from an unknown source some distance away. As I walked back to my accommodation unit I was struck by another. When I arrived back at the unit and had washed the egg goo off myself I laughingly told one of the other older inmates about it. 'Some of these chaps are very young and very bored. I suppose we must expect pranks like that from time to time?'

'That's no fucking prank mate, that's a fucking warning, they are telling you to go and ask to be taken back to Cessnock into the protection unit. If you don't you're fucked!' he cautioned me seriously. 'It's out of the question,' I replied firmly. 'I am not going to run to the guards like a girl and ask to be taken to the protection wing at Cessnock Prison where I am locked in a cell most of the day just because some boys threw a couple of eggs at me. I am not that fragile.'

'Suit yourself then. You're fucked then!' he informed me.

I had four more eggs thrown at me over the next two days and on the third day a large young boy came into my cell and punched me half a dozen times before telling me 'You better fuck off, we don't want you here.'

Half an hour later as I was standing at the sink in the bathroom cleaning myself up one of the real tough men of the prison who I had never had personal interaction with, came into the bathroom and looked at me. 'I have just heard what happened,' he said. 'They have no right to pick on an old man like you, it's not right, don't worry I will sort it out.'

I have no idea how he sorted it out but in the short term there were no more attacks. Notwithstanding this respite I always understood that as the underlying resentment hadn't changed so I was still at risk. To mitigate the risk I limited my movements to and from my room and always asked someone else to walk or run with me during my daily exercise. It was an awful and anxious time for me.

On 22 May, some eight and a half weeks after my arrival, my classification was changed and I was moved out into the Dumaresq compound and the risk of violence abated substantially. Muswellbrook Prison has accommodation for a total of 260 inmates. About 160 are housed, as I had first been, in the hostels units inside the high security wire fence but the remaining 100 low risk prisoners are housed in similar but slightly better units in an special purpose unfenced compound just outside the prison wire called Dumaresq.

The purpose of the Dumaresq compound is to provide a graduated transition for inmates from prison life to the outside world when they are in the last months or weeks of their sentences. Although all inmates are mustered and counted several times each day then locked away in the hostel units overnight there is some trust involved as there is no wire – an enthusiastic inmate could theoretically escape during the day between muster counts.

Many of these inmates are also allowed limited day leave then weekend leave to spend time and become reconnected with their families prior to their release.

On 10 and 11 June, Kristine came to visit me for the second time since my arrest. It was wonderful to spend time with her and I really felt that our future together as a couple had every prospect of success. I was pleased to advise her that my divorce from Sheila had become final on 6 June and as soon as she felt willing and able I hoped she would remarry me with proper legal formality and spend her life with me. She did not agree to marry me but she said that in time if complete trust could be restored she felt certain we could remarry.

During my whole time in Muswellbrook Prison Kristine wrote me 200 letters and spoke with me 190 times on the telephone. She really did offer support to me.

Just after Kristine's visit I was offered a prison job change from the clerk in the vegetable processing factory to clerk down on the farm and jumped at it. Although this job also included payroll for inmates working on the farm there were far fewer workers and their pay status and hours of work were far more stable so their were very few requests for unauthorised pay rises and bonuses.

My first primary task was to calculate vegetable demand from forward orders then purchase vegetables from external suppliers for the vegetable processing factory. My second primary task was to calculate meat demand from forward orders that came from four different prisons then prepare buying orders for cattle to be bought at various sale yards at changing market prices before being sent to different abattoirs then to the cold store we had at the prison farm prior to dispatch to the prisons on the due dates. My third primary task was to process all the paperwork to ensure suppliers were paid and to maintain basic accounting records that calculated the profit and loss of the unit.

I have almost no personal agricultural experience but the 480-hectare farm was obviously run without regard to basic commercial principles. When the prison farm manager was not involved in preparing or eating lunch he spent a great deal of his time at the stables where two inmates cared for the daily needs of about 10 Clydesdale horses and a racehorse owned by a syndicate of prison officers that he was involved in. 'Why do we keep Clydesdale horses on the farm?' I asked the prison farm manager. 'They don't appear to have any practical agricultural function, we don't breed and sell them at a profit, and they just seem to be a costly overhead.'

'We have them for education so we can train inmates about horses,' he replied confidently. 'But we only ever have two inmates at the stables, they change perhaps three times a year so no more than eight inmates a year out of the 260 here even get near the horses. It doesn't seem a very cost effective or sensible education program to me,' I replied cautiously.

'That's because you are a fucking criminal and don't know anything!' he replied with a confident chuckle.

Apart from the inmates looking after the horses at any given time half a dozen inmates were involved in growing and harvesting a small crop of vegetables in the most arable part of the farm. Most of the remaining land was used for grazing beef cattle but as the property had very little grass there were often two people deployed on feeding the cattle grain and hay at a significant cost. Many of the fences on the farm were in poor repair and nine cattle had recently died on the farm due to various misadventures.

'This whole operation is a failure at just about every level and a huge waste of the taxpayer's money,' I chastised the prison farm manager.

'Don't be so critical of me Harry. You will be coming back to prison you know,' he informed me.

'What on earth makes you think that?' I asked him incredulously.

'Well! You are excessively bossy in your dealings with me for a start. You are always at me to do this or do that as if you run the place. Don't you understand you are a now just a disgraceful criminal with no place in society.'

The Saturday after her weekly visit Josaphine and I again discussed her precarious personal situation. She had abandoned her job, car, furniture, etc. in Brunei in November, some seven months ago. For the first four months after her return she had been under bail conditions and embroiled in her own legal problems so that she was unable to work. Although she not paying rent to live in our home in North Arm Cove she had been obliged to pay for a couple of expensive maintenance costs amounting to thousands of dollars such as replacing the main water supply pump so her accommodation had not been free. Our North Arm Cove home was in an isolated rural location so the cost of travel to town each week was significant. Her weekly visits to me each Saturday cost about $150 in fuel and sundry costs. Both she and her boyfriend, who was living with her, had been receiving unemployment payments but that didn't come close to covering her costs and she had now used up the last of her cash reserves.

Since the charges against her had been dropped she had tried without success to secure employment locally, not just as a high school teacher but any sort of clerical work. 'I am 30 years old Daddy, I have never worked in a shop or as a clerk and because of the stuff the police media unit pumped out about me I have a high public profile locally as a criminal. I don't know if I can ever get a job locally.'

In due course the NSW Education Department offered her a temporary posting in the remote western country centre of Parkes, about six hours drive away. It was inconvenient, isolated and difficult mostly because it was such a long drive for her to visit me in prison but it was a job so she accepted it, found a flat for herself and Chriseb in Parkes and started work there in late July.

On Saturday 29 July, after she started living and working in Parkes I was allowed my first eight-hour day leave in the township of Muswellbrook. Josaphine and Chriseb had to leave

Parkes at 2.00am and drive for six and a half hours in order to collect me at 8.30 in the morning. We had a swim in the local pool together followed by a meal at McDonald's then just walked and talked together in a local park. It was wonderful to be out of the prison environment even for a few hours and I was very grateful for the time, cost and effort Josaphine spent to make it happen for me. In accordance with the program guidelines I was allowed another local day leave two weeks later then another two weeks after that and each time and Josaphine, Chriseb and I spent a glorious day together at Lake Glenbawn, just out of Muswellbrook.

My first weekend leave was approved for the weekend of 9 and 10 September and again required a huge sacrifice in time, effort and cost from Josaphine in order to collect and take me to and from our North Arm Cove home for the weekend although neither she nor Chriseb spent any time there with me. Kristine had arranged to fly from New Zealand and come to our North Arm Cove home to spend the first weekend leave with me and didn't want to share my time.

'It seems just a little selfish that on your first weekend leave she can't allow a couple of hours for us all to spend together as a family!' Josaphine protested mildly but she facilitated the visit with just a shake of her head.

It was wonderful for Kristine and me to have the time together as a couple and of course to share a bed together again as lovers. I was allowed more weekend leave on 23 and 24 September, then every weekend until my release from prison. Although we had many visits and telephone calls from friends during these weekends at home the many hours I spent alone with Josaphine and Chriseb more than compensated for the weekend that had been given exclusively to Kristine.

'Ha,' Josaphine snorted indignantly when I talked about

it. 'That's all well and good, but she is supposed to be my stepmother and Chriseb's step-grandmother, it wouldn't have hurt her to make time for us either!'

The weekend leave program rules did not allow me to leave the grounds of my home except to travel to and from the prison unless a special purpose excursion, up to four hours, was applied for and granted. I applied for and was granted two excursions. The first allowed me a three-hour excursion into the local village to have a haircut and on another I was allowed extra travel time home on the Saturday morning for me to stop at an optometrist and have my eyes tested for spectacles. Once my weekend leave started although I continued to stay in prison during the week I really stopped feeling like a prisoner and I was just marking time until my release.

I had a rude awakening on my last weekend leave on 28 October. Josaphine had been on time to collect me as always but for some reason it took about 15 minutes longer for me to be processed and leave the prison than normal. On the journey home we got held up in traffic for another 15-minute delay when a wide load blocked the road for a while as it passed through a village.

As was our habit we also stopped at a McDonald's and had a half-hour coffee break to give Josaphine a little rest from driving as she had already driven for more than six and a half hours before she collected me. When we reached Raymond Terrace we stopped for perhaps another 15 minutes to pick up bread, milk and a few essential items from a petrol station convenience store. When we reached Karuah Josaphine stopped at the local post office to collect our mail and was delayed again because the postmistress had ducked next door for a few minutes on a personal errand. With one thing and another we reached our North Cove home in four and a half hours instead of the three and a half hours allowed for the journey. The prison service had made a routine phone call to check that I had arrived on the scheduled arrival time and left a message on the telephone answering machine to call as soon as I arrived.

I telephoned the prison and was informed that my late arrival was a breach of the rules and was instructed to return to prison immediately. Upon my return as my punishment I was formally charged with breaking the rules and had to appear before two senior officers. I was placed in solitary confinement for the last week of my sentence as my punishment.

One of the unintended consequences of my hurried trip back to the prison and spending the last week in solitary was that I had no opportunity to arrange any civilian clothing for my release. I knew I could keep and wear the prison-green T-shirt with a collar I was wearing because I had bought it myself to get the collar as one of my Dumaresq buy-up privileges along with a pair of Puma sneakers. I was wearing socks and underpants that Josaphine had provided me but I had no pants of my own.

At 8.30am on the morning of my scheduled release with a minimum of delay I was taken from my cell to reception by a senior officer. 'I know you will fuck up again and be back in prison again, your type always comes back and I just hope I am here when you do come back so I can make your fucking miserable life worse you fucking low life!'

After his little speech I was quickly processed before being given a lift into town. A little after 9.00am wearing only my green shirt, underpants and socks with sneakers I was dropped in the main street of Muswellbrook with a small folder containing my release papers.

17

Postscript

APRIL 2007

On 5 November, I was driven from the prison into Muswellbrook by a prison officer and released in the main street.

My first action as a free man was to find a public phone and call Josaphine. She advised me that a lot had happened in the last week I had been in prison. I had planned to spend a couple of weeks at North Arm with my new wife Kristine after my release from prison until I found my bearings.

During this first free telephone conversation with Josaphine she told me that she was unable to come and collect me as she didn't have a car and for various reasons we couldn't go to North Arm.

Josaphine said she had made alternative arrangements for me and within 20 minutes of my release I was located and collected in the main street of Muswellbrook by Kristine. She had flown over from New Zealand and then driven up from

Sydney with my old friends Charlie and Diane. After a loving roadside greeting from Kristine we climbed into the car and Diane passed me a couple of basic outfits of clothing she had bought for me to wear before driving to their home on the central coast.

Charlie and Diane had a self-contained unit on the second floor of their home and they made it available for our exclusive use. The 'honeymoon suite' as Charlie called it. Charlie had also arranged for a new car for our personal use for as long as we needed it and offered to provide us with any immediate money we may need. Their generosity, hospitality and kindness were quite breathtaking. Kristine and I spent the rest of the day alone making love, talking and eating all the delicacies that Charlie and Diane had prepared for us. It was wonderful for us to be together again.

Before my disappearance I had a longstanding commercial relationship with the entertainment agency Markson Sparks. Over many years they had provided our group of companies with public speakers and entertainers for various corporate functions. A couple of weeks before my release on one of my weekend leaves I had contacted Max, the proprietor of Markson Sparks, and explained that since my arrest Kristine had received many requests for paid interviews from various media organisations. There was no reason why Kristine should not accept some to help ends meet. I also was happy to be interviewed but did not accept any money as I understood that it would be unwise for me to accept any payments due to the 'proceeds of crime' legislation.

Apart from those media engagements for Kristine and a couple of public-speaking engagements for myself we had no set plans or obligations for a month except to enjoy each other's company. After a couple of days at Charlie and Diane's home we drove down to Sydney in the car Charlie provided and spent time visiting the many friends who had supported me during my incarceration. We were wined, dined and accommodated wherever we went and there were many random acts of kindness. For example, Tania and Michael welcomed us into their Sydney home and felt that we could use some time alone and provided us with their beach home on the south coast for as long as we needed it.

One day we went out on Sydney Harbour as guests of our agent Max on his motor launch. In a typically multi-tasking activity he talked to me as he drank his wine while steering the launch and answering text messages on his phone. It all proved too much for him as he accidentally ran the launch onto some rocks at Watsons Bay. His brother David and I were ordered overboard to lighten the load as he gingerly reversed the launch off the rocks.

'Do be careful!' he admonished me as I treaded water.

'Nobody will ever believe me if I tell them you have been lost overboard again, they will think it is just an agent's publicity stunt!' It was a wonderful day out and we often refer to it in conversation with friends as our brush with the rich and famous.

November seemed to pass in a blur: visiting friends, meeting the media, speaking engagements, eating too much, walking hand in hand on beaches and loving each other. It was a wonderful time for us both, although the stress of contact with the police, then obtaining a new passport for me weighed heavily on Kristine from time to time.

On 3 December with my new passport in my hand Kristine and I flew back to Auckland, New Zealand. We were collected at the airport by one of Kristine's daughters and her family. I faced a daunting list of domestic tasks that had backed up. I quickly fixed the drainage problem, constructed and painted a new front fence, painted the house, planted countless trees and shrubs and well as seeing to many other minor tasks. Kristine's first colour selection for the house was pink but when I had painted two walls I started to answer the phone with 'Barbie's house, Ken speaking' so she changed the colour to purple. It now has a silver roof, purple walls; magenta trim, black base and I think it looks a real treat.

Kristine and I spend most of our time in Auckland, where I have taken up a part-time marketing position with a property development company. Although our primary residence and commercial interests are in Auckland I spend a significant amount of time in Sydney each month for both personal and commercial reasons. It isn't difficult to divide my time between my Australian and New Zealand commercial interests, but Kristine and I loathe spending time apart and in the long term we will seek to limit the travel and time apart.

Kristine and I continue to enjoy a rich and loving emotional life together as a couple. We share every aspect of married life and are committed to each other in every way. Although I lost most of my former wealth I returned to commercial life with an adequate income for our needs.

My daughter Lisa and I write to each other frequently and I am proud to acknowledge her publicly as my daughter. No DNA test will ever be required.

Kristine continues to enjoy the love and affection of her two daughters, but sadly has become estranged from her son who is a London policeman.

All of my siblings exchanged polite supportive letters with me during the time I was in prison, but we have not maintained contact since my release. Any real emotional relationship with Josaphine, Chriseb and me would be incompatible with the close and continuing relationships they each have with Sheila.

Although I am saddened by the loss Josaphine feels it more keenly than I do because I am now the only living relative she and Chriseb have any contact with.

Sheila continues to reside in our Surry Hills home and the North Arm Cove home remains empty. I don't have or seek any information on her emotional and financial life as it really is none of my business. I do hope that sometime before she dies that she telephones Josaphine and asks to be reconciled with her. It would be difficult for both of them to find a common pathway but Josaphine is her only child, Chriseb is her only grandchild and she is their only mother and grandmother. Most worthwhile results in life require real risk and effort.

For my part, the price I have paid for this whole adventure is a feeling that I will never ever feel safe again.

Although I love Kristine dearly, there is a sense that I need to treat all conversations with her as if they may at some time be repeated to a policeman and/or appear in a newspaper.

In my exchange of letters with my siblings and friends I don't consider my correspondence to be private and confidential. There will never be a shared private emotional space in my life ever again. If my car was stolen or my home was burgled I feel I could never go to the police as I am now fair game to be charged with whatever they feel they can get away with if I come to their attention again.

I have plenty of love and friendship in my life and I should be grateful for that.

18

Final chapter

After my release from prison I wrote a book then I settled into a life of quiet industry. I worked hard to build two successful businesses in Australia employing more than 20 people and we have lived a quiet and uncontroversial life.

I have now disposed of all my business interests and both my wife and I are happily retired. We are by no means super rich but we are more than financially secure and have the means and time to enjoy the arts. When this pandemic passes we will travel more. In 2019, before the pandemic, we toured Japan together and were delighted by the sights and delights of that country that we knew little of. We would like to do more of that. To look, learn and wonder.

My wife, Kristine, has deep family ties in New Zealand so prior to Covid-19 we shuttled between our homes in Sydney and Auckland, often on a monthly basis. Each time I arrived at our Auckland home I would raise the Australian flag on the flagpole in our front yard and sing 'Advance Australia Fair' at full voice. I am so, so Australian. Like all other Australians and perhaps all humans, my life and ability to travel changed and I spent most of 2020 in Australia with my wife away from me in Auckland. As soon as the travel bubble opened up this year I was able to joyfully reunite with my wife. My daughter and grandson still live in Australia so I will continue to commute, but being more mindful of my carbon footprint and climate change these days I will travel less frequently. When my grandson completed high school I advised him to become a plumbing apprentice in one of my businesses. Who ever met a poor plumber? He decided instead to go to university and do commerce. In 2020 the universities closed their doors and I understand that provided him the time and opportunity to pursue his romantic interests. Who knows where that will all end?

My former wife died in April 2017 of lung cancer and I have reflected on the fact that I managed to quit smoking when I was 40 years old but she couldn't rid herself of that awful drug and it probably killed her. How very sad. We had many differences but she had many qualities that I admired then and now.

Pilots learn in their flying training that every extra level of stress leads to worse decision-making. Not a good thing up in the air. Although I had a happy personal and commercial life in 1999 with more than enough money, homes and possessions I was under a great deal of stress in 2000 and made a very bad decision to fake my death to escape my problems. It was stupid at every level but that does not define me as a stupid person. I was under a great deal of stress and made a very stupid decision. I acknowledge that I am an international disgrace but I still have love, financial security from my own efforts and an interesting life now.

As a child I remember my father reciting this mantra:
'The loss of time is much,
The loss of money more,
But the loss of reputation can never be restored.'

211

My story does not have an unhappy ending but I know I will always be damaged. With hard work I have managed to put life back together so that I am a functional and even worthwhile human being but I am and will always be damaged. 'The loss of reputation can never be restored.'